FOREST LAND USE:

AN ANNOTATED BIBLIOGRAPHY

OF

POLICY, ECONOMIC, AND MANAGEMENT ISSUES

1970-1980

A Conservation Foundation Report

This report was prepared under a grant from the Weyerhaeuser
Company Foundation; however, The Conservation Foundation is
responsible for the selection of works in the bibliography and
the description of their content.

This bibliography was compiled by William E. Shands, Senior Associate at The Conservation Foundation, with the assistance of Barbara K. Rodes, Research Librarian, and Noreen O'Meara, Research Assistant. Bernice Hudson typed the many drafts and with the assistance of Jenny Billet assembled the final manuscript for publication. Cover artwork and design was done by Michael Rawson.

FOREST LAND USE: AN ANNOTATED BIBLIOGRAPHY OF POLICY, ECONOMIC, AND MANAGEMENT ISSUES, 1970-1980

Copyright © 1981 by The Conservation Foundation

Library of Congress Catalog Card Number: 81-68375

International Standard Book Number: 0-89164-067-3

All rights reserved. No part of this book may be reproduced in any form without the permission of The Conservation Foundation.

The Conservation Foundation
1717 Massachusetts Avenue, N.W.
Washington, D.C. 20036

CONTENTS

	Page
PREFACE	ix
INTRODUCTION	xi

I. LAND USE POLICY - GENERAL 1

<u>The Quiet Revolution in Land Use Control</u> - Fred Bosselman and David Callies (1971)............................ 1

<u>The Taking Issue: An Analysis of the Constitutional Limits of Land Use Control</u> - Fred Bosselman, David Callies, and John Banta (1973)............ 2

<u>Perspectives on Prime Land: Background Papers for Seminar on Retention of Prime Lands</u> - U.S. Department of Agriculture (1975)..................... 3

<u>Subdividing Rural America: Impacts of Recreational Lot and Second Home Development</u> - American Society of Planning Officials (1976)..................... 4

<u>Untaxing Open Space - An Evaluation of the Effectiveness of Differential Assessment of Farms and Open Space</u> - John C. Keene, <u>et.al</u>. (1976)................... 5

<u>Land Use and the States</u> - Robert G. Healy and John S. Rosenberg (1979)................. 6

II. FOREST LAND USE ISSUES AND POLICY 7

<u>One Third of the Nation's Land : A Report to the President and to the Congress</u> - Public Land Law Review Commission (1970)............................. 7

<u>Forest Policy for the Future: Conflict, Compromise, Consensus</u> - Marion Clawson, Editor (1974).. 9

	Page

Forests For Whom and For What? -
Marion Clawson (1975).................................. 10

Proceedings of the Forest Taxation
Symposium, November 30-December 1,
1977, Blacksburg, Virginia - Harry L.
Haney and John E. Gunter, Editors
(1978)... 11

Forestry and Long Range Planning -
Frank J. Convery and Charles W.
Ralston, Editors (1977)............................... 13

Centers of Influence and U.S. Forest
Policy - Frank J. Convery and Jean E.
Davis, Editors (1977)................................. 14

The Yankee Forest: A Prospectus -
Carl H. Reidel (1978)................................. 14

Forest and Range Policy: Its Development
in the United States - Sally K. Fairfax
and Samuel Trask Dana (1980).......................... 15

III. FOREST PRODUCTS SUPPLY AND DEMAND........................ 17

Final Report - President's Advisory
Panel on Timber and the Environment
(1973).. 17

Man, Materials and Environment
National Academy of Sciences/
National Academy of Engineering (1973)............... 19

Is Timber Scarce? The Economics of a
Renewable Resource - Lloyd C. Irland
(1974).. 19

An Assessment of the Forest and Range-
Land Situation in the United States
U.S. Department of Agriculture,
Forest Service (1980)................................. 20

Analysis of the Timber Situation in the
United States, 1952-2030-- Review Draft
U.S. Department of Agriculture,
Forest Service (1980)................................. 22

Forest Productivity Report - Forest
Industries Council (1980)............................. 23

  Page

IV. ECONOMIC ANALYSIS 25

     The Economics of Natural Environments:
         Studies in the Valuation of Commodity
         and Amenity Resources - John V.
         Krutilla and Anthony C. Fisher (1975)............... 25

     Decision Making in Timber Production,
         Harvest and Marketing - Marion Clawson
         (1977).. 26

     Unpriced Values: Decisions Without
         Market Prices - John A. Sinden and
         Albert C. Worrell (1979)............................ 27

     Timber Supply, Land Allocation, and
         Economic Efficiency - William F. Hyde
         (1980).. 29

V.   MANAGEMENT OF FOREST RESOURCES 31

     Methods for Identifying and Evaluating
         the Nature and Extent of Nonpoint
         Sources of Pollutants - U.S. Environ-
         mental Protection Agency, Office of
         Air and Water Programs (1973)....................... 31

     Forest Resource Management: Decision-
         Making Principles and Cases - William A.
         Duerr, et. al., Editors (1975)...................... 32

     Impacts of Large Recreational Developments
         Upon Semi-Primitive Environments: The
         Gallatin Canyon Synthesis Report -
         Gallatin Canyon Study Team, University of Montana
         (1976).. 32

     Management of Eastern Hardwood Forests
         for Multiple Benefits (DYNAST-MB) -
         Stephen G. Boyce (1977)............................. 33

     Wilderness Management - John C. Hendee,
         et.al. (1977)....................................... 34

     Wildlife Habitat in Managed Forests - The
         Blue Mountains of Oregon and Washington
         Jack Ward Thomas, Technical Editor (1979)........... 35

	Page

VI. **NATIONAL FOREST POLICY** 37

    <u>Crisis in Federal Forest Land Management</u> - Dennis C. LeMaster and Luke Popovich, Editors (1977).................................... 37

    <u>The Lands Nobody Wanted: Policy for National Forests in the Eastern United States</u> - William E. Shands and Robert G. Healy (1977).......................... 38

    <u>An Integrated Approach to National Forest Management</u> - John V. Krutilla and John A. Haigh (1978).............................. 38

    <u>The National Forests-Better Planning Needed to Improve Resource Management</u> - U.S. General Accounting Office (1978)............. 39

    <u>Federal Resource Lands and Their Neighbors</u> - William E. Shands (1979)............... 39

    <u>National Forest Policy: From Conflict Toward Consensus</u> - William E. Shands, Perry R. Hagenstein, and Marissa T. Roche (1979)....................................... 40

VII. **POLICY FOR NON-INDUSTRIAL PRIVATE FORESTS**............. 43

    <u>The Challenge of Private Woodlands: The Report of the Trees for People Task Force</u> - Kenneth B. Pomeroy and John Muench (1975).................................. 43

    <u>Policy Alternatives for Nonindustrial Private Forests</u> - Roger A. Sedjo and David M. Ostermeier (1978)........................ 44

    <u>The Economics of U.S. Nonindustrial Private Forests</u> - Marion Clawson (1979)............ 45

    "Timber Supply From Private Non-industrial Forests: An Economic Analysis" - Clark Shepard Binkley (1979)....................... 46

    <u>America Grows on Trees: The Promise of Private, Nonindustrial Woodlands</u> - National Forest Products Association (1980).. 47

Page

    <u>Proceedings of the National Private
Non-Industrial Forestry Conference</u>
National Association of State
Foresters and U.S. Department of
Agriculture, Forest Service (1981).................. 49

VIII. FORESTRY RESEARCH 51

    <u>Report of the Committee on Research
Advisory to the U.S. Department of
Agriculture</u> - National Academy of
Sciences (1972)...................................... 51

    <u>Renewable Resources for Industrial
Materials</u> - National Academy of Sciences
(1976)... 52

    <u>Research in Forest Economics and Forest
Policy</u> - Marion Clawson, Editor (1977)............. 54

    <u>National Program of Research for Forests
and Associated Rangeland</u> - Ronald D.
Lindmark and Mason E. Miller, Editors (1978)....... 55

IX. INTERNATIONAL FORESTRY 57

    <u>Forest Management in Canada</u> - F.L.C. Reed
and Associates (1978).............................. 57

    <u>Papers for Conference on Improved
Utilization of Tropical Forests</u> -
U.S. Department of Agriculture, Forest
Service, Forest Products Laboratory
(1978)... 58

    <u>Planting for the Future: Forestry for
Human Needs</u> - Erik Eckholm (1979)................. 58

    <u>The World's Tropical Forests: A Policy,
Strategy, and Program for the United
States</u> - U.S. Interagency Task Force
on Tropical Forests (1980)......................... 59

    <u>Forest Activities and Deforestation
Problems in Developing Countries</u>
John I. Zerbe, <u>et. al.</u> (1980)..................... 60

    <u>The Global 2000 Report to the President:
Entering the Twenty-First Century</u> -
Council on Environmental Quality/
Department of State (1980)......................... 61

PREFACE

The Conservation Foundation prepared this report as an information source for the Weyerhaeuser Company Foundation's Land Use Advisory Committee--to provide the committee with information on significant conferences, other meetings, and research conducted on forest land use over the past decade. The report is not intended as a comprehensive bibliography, but should provide the committee and other readers with an idea of the significant research directions and major policy issues that have emerged over the past ten years. In preparing this annotated bibliography, we chose selections which met at least one of three criteria:

1. Those meetings and studies which have resulted in major forest land use policy changes, either in terms of legislation or programs in the public or private sectors.

2. Those meetings and studies which have made a significant contribution to the exploration of major forest policy issues.

3. Those efforts, primarily in research and analysis, which represent the leading edge of thought on or study of major forest land use issues.

In this work, we surveyed more than 70 reports and proceedings of meetings, and selected about 50 for discussion. Major sections of this paper deal with land use issues generally, forest land and resource management and use, national forest management, non-industrial private forests, economic analysis and methodologies, research, and international developments. In the interests of space we have omitted some studies that were important in their time if later works on the same subject have included most of their findings and gone beyond them; thus in a swiftly changing field most of the material covered is from the last half of the decade.

Readers are likely to note the absence of a discrete section on industrial forest land issues. We did, in fact, seek to develop a section dealing specifically with issues of industrial land ownership and use, and consulted widely with persons at the Weyerhaeuser Company, the National Forest Products Association, and others. However, there is a paucity of material dealing specifically with industrial forest land. The reasons for this, in our view, are three. First, there is general agreement that the forest industry is managing its land at a much higher level of timber productivity than that achieved by the Forest Service for the National Forests, or by small landowners for their land; thus major studies understandably deal with what researchers see as the two "problem" areas. Second, decisions about industrial forest management policy are appropriately made by the companies themselves in accordance with company economic objectives, and industrial forest land policy is not considered an appropriate field for governmental action; thus, the industrial forests have not attracted academic research nor served as the basis for policy meetings, as have the National Forests and non-industrial private forests. Finally, much of the information required for policy analysis is proprietary in nature and closely guarded by the individual companies or, conversely, is held in confidentiality because of anti-trust implications; thus much industry data are not available for public analysis.

While we were unable to locate any studies or reports dealing specifically with industrial forest land use, several of the works reviewed in this paper do have sections addressing industrial sector issues, along with consideration of National Forest policy or policy for non-industrial private forests. Notable among these are Marion Clawson's Timber Production, Harvest and Marketing, the National Academy of Sciences' Renewable Resources for Industrial Materials, and some of the papers in Forestry and Long Range Planning, published by Duke University's School of Forestry and Environmental Studies. Significantly, the editors of that volume urged that "forest industry planners and managers commit their ideas more frequently to print. If 'publish or perish' is the watchword for academicians, 'publish and perish' seems to be the guiding sentiment among their counterparts in industry."

Some of the studies and reports have stimulated the enactment of specific legislation; the report of the Public Land Law Review Commission is probably the best example of this type. Others have advanced ideas which, over time, have been worked into legislation and policy--Clawson's advocacy of intensive management of high-site class timber land on the National Forests is a prime example. Others, such as the Forest Service RPA Assessment, are standard sources of information for policy makers and resource planners. Other studies simply develop methodologies for economic analysis or determining management regimes to accomplish specific objectives. However, with the exception of the few that can be explicitly linked to specific legislation, policy, or programs, the impacts of these studies cannot be determined objectively.

In the course of reviewing works for inclusion in this paper, we received a number of suggestions from the Weyerhaesuer Company, reviewed most of them, and included many. However, the materials covered here represent those The Conservation Foundation believes to be of significance.

In the body of this paper, the reports are arranged chronologically--from earliest to most recent, within each subject area.

INTRODUCTION: THE NATION'S FOREST LAND*

Of the nation's 2.3 billion acres of land, 740.2 million acres--about one third--are forest land (defined as land at least 10 percent occupied by forest trees of any size, or formerly having had such tree cover and not presently in another use).

Of these 740.2 million acres, 487.7 million acres are classified as commercial forest lands--lands "capable of producing industrial crops of wood [20 cubic feet per acre per year] and not withdrawn by statute or administrative regulation." The remainder, 252.4 million acres, are classified as non-commercial forest lands--lands incapable of or unavailable for growing trees for harvest.

Of the 252.4 million acres of non-commercial forest lands, 228.3 million acres are considered unproductive or presently incapable of growing enough wood fiber per acre to make them profitable for harvest (of this, 107 million acres are in Alaska). The remaining 24.2 million acres of non-commercial forest land are classified as either productive reserved or deferred--including land in parks and wilderness areas or other areas where timber-harvesting is prohibited.

---

* Material in this section has been condensed from the American Forest Institute pamphlet "Forest Facts and Figures." Data for the pamphlet, according to AFI, were drawn from "Forest Statistics, 1977," published by the USDA Forest Service, and other Forest Service publications. Some of these data have been updated by the 1980 Analysis of the Timber Situation in the United States; see page 22.

Nearly three-fourths of all commercial forest land is located in the Eastern half of the country, about equally divided between the North and South. (See Map)

REGIONS OF THE UNITED STATES
(As defined in "Forest Facts and Figures,"
American Forest Institute)

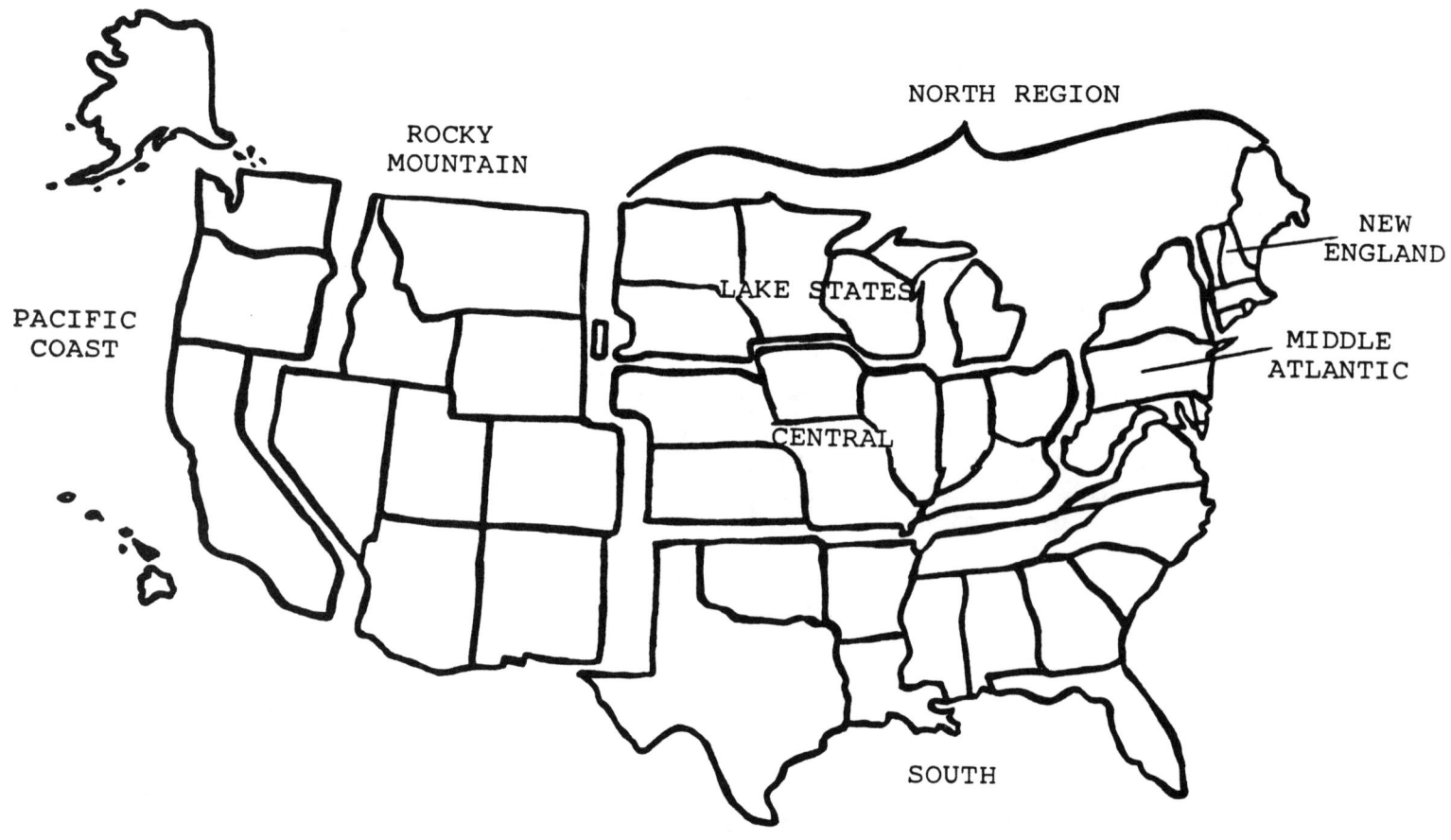

About 77 percent of New England, more than half of the land along the Atlantic Coast, nearly one fourth of the Lake States, and 14 percent of the Central Region are covered with commercial forests. Data on forested land by region follow.

LAND AREAS BY REGION, JANUARY 1, 1977
(1,000 acres)

Region	Total Land Area	Total Forest Land	Percent Forested	Commercial Forest Land	Productive Reserved Forest Land	Productive Deferred Forest Land	Other Forest
North							
New England	40,289	32,491	81	31,015	485	25	967
Mid-Atlantic	87,207	51,852	60	48,215	2,944	36	657
Lake States	208,033	53,270	26	49,984	991	36	2,259
Central	291,633	43,229	15	41,556	718	56	899
Total	627,161	180,842	29	170,769	5,138	153	4,782
South	510,777	207,072	41	188,433	1,871	101	16,667
Pacific Coast	570,862	214,487	38	70,758	4,132	1,189	138,408
Rocky Mountain	554,748	137,747	25	57,765	8,390	3,183	68,408
Total All Regions	2,263,548	740,147	33	487,726	19,531	4,626	228,264

The federal government is the largest single owner of commercial forest lands. The 187-million-acre National Forest System contains 89 million acres of commercial forest (18 percent of all commercial forest land). The bulk of this commercial forest land is in the Pacific Coast and Rocky Mountain regions. Other federal agencies, including the Bureau of Land Management, manage 10.7 million acres, or two percent of commercial forest land. States, counties, municipalities, and Indian tribes own another 36.9 million acres of commercial forest land (8 percent of total).

The forest products industry owns 68 million acres of commercial forest land, or 14 percent of the total. Of this, 53 percent is in the South, 26 percent in the North, and most of the rest on the Pacific Coast.

But the greatest portion of commercial forest land--283.1 million acres, or 58 percent--is owned by individuals. Nearly half of these lands are in the South and most of the rest are in the North. These are the non-industrial private forests, and while classified as commercial forest land and thus capable of producing crops of industrial wood, there is evidence that only a small percentage of the land is actually owned and managed to produce timber for sale. Forest land ownership by section follows.

AREAS OF COMMERCIAL FOREST LAND IN THE U.S. BY OWNERSHIP, 1977
(1,000 acres)

Region	Total All Ownerships	National Forests	Other Federal	Other Public, Indian, State, County and Municipal	Forest Industry	Other Private
North						
New England	31,015	706	64	1,088	9,898	19,259
Mid-Atlantic	48,215	1,338	180	4,474	2,855	39,368
Lake States	49,984	5,672	327	13,749	4,219	26,017
Central	41,556	2,406	523	792	805	37,030
Total	170,769	10,121	1,094	20,103	17,777	121,674
South	188,433	10,955	3,346	3,442	35,754	134,937
Pacific Coast	70,758	31,496	4,465	8,414	12,349	14,035
Rocky Mountain	57,765	36,436	1,743	4,989	2,096	12,502
Total All Regions	487,726	89,007	10,648	36,947	67,976	283,149

After World War II, up until about 1960, the extent of the nation's commercial timberland grew as farmland returned to forest, particularly in the East. However, the trend reversed during the 1960s and 1970s. From 1962 to 1977, the commercial forest land base declined by 23.3 million acres, with most of the loss in the South and Rocky Mountain states. The causes of the decline were the shift of forest land to reserved or deferred status while under consideration for wilderness or recreational area designation, increased use of forest land for roads and rights of way, urban expansion, and--particularly in the South--the conversion of forest land to cropland and reservoirs. At this writing, the Congress is considering a number of proposals to establish Wilderness Areas on the National Forests, and the Forest Service is in the midst of intensive planning for the National Forests; both of these activities will effect the amount of commercial forest land available.

I: Land Use Policy - General

In the late 1960's and early 1970's, there was a surge of interest in land use planning at the state or regional levels. Also, President Nixon proposed a National Land Use Policy Act which would have provided federal grants to states for land use planning and regulation. Several of the reports reviewed in this section deal with the question of which level of government should make land use decisions. Another addresses a prime constitutional issue involved in land use regulation. Two others deal with perceived threats to traditional uses of rural land, and another with methods of preserving open space through tax incentives. None of the selections deals exclusively or even principally with forest lands, but all do establish the policy contexts in which many decisions affecting the conversion of forest land to other uses are made.

Bosselman, Fred, and Callies, David. The Quiet Revolution in Land Use Control. Prepared for the Council on Environmental Quality. Washington, D.C.: U.S. Government Printing Office, 1971. 327pp.

This report was published during Congressional debate on the Nixon Administration's proposed National Land Use Policy Act, which sparked controversy over government's (especially the federal government's) role in land use decisions. Although Congress did not enact the national land use legislation, many states had previously passed their own land use laws which provided for a measure of state control over activity in certain critical areas such as wetlands, coastal areas, and areas where large-scale regional development was taking place. The report analyzes innovative state land use laws in order to focus attention on how the more complex land use issues, including pollution, wetlands preservation, and large-scale development, were being addressed at the state and local levels.

Today it is largely outdated; but for a time this publication served as a working manual for states, such as Florida and Colorado, which were developing land use and environmental legislation. Most of the laws discussed--the Hawaiian land use law, Vermont's Environmental Control Law, and others--have been modified, and many new ones have been instituted. California and Oregon are still in the throes of implementing their large-scale land use plans, one for coastal areas, the other a comprehensive land use plan. The issues surrounding federal, state, and local roles in land use decision-making outlined in the report have shifted as well. Currently, the trend is away from state agency implementation of land use laws and toward reliance on local governments to implement state-mandated laws.

Bosselman, Fred; Callies, David; and Banta, John. *The Taking Issue: An Analysis of the Constitutional Limits of Land Use Control.* Prepared for the Council on Environmental Quality. Washington, D.C.: U.S. Government Printing Office, 1973. 329pp.

Written in 1973, when many states and local governments were using their police powers to regulate land use decisions to enhance environmental quality, *The Taking Issue* has become a classic in land use law.

The study focuses on the constraint upon the regulation of land use by government found in the "taking clause" of the Fifth Amendment to the United States Constitution, which states: "...nor shall private property be taken for public use without just compensation." The report traces the distinction between a valid regulation of the use of land and a "taking" that requires compensation. The authors provide detailed documentation, since their work was intended as a technical resource book for attorneys and government officials. Among the authors' findings are the following:

- the taking clause is a serious problem for land regulating agencies wherever there is substantial pressure for urban growth;

- "...fear of the taking issue is stronger than the taking clause itself";

- there is little historical basis for the idea that a regulation of the use of land can constitute a taking of land;

- court decisions of the early 1970's strongly support land use regulations based on overall state or regional goals.

The trend identified in the report toward judicial upholding of land use regulations continues. Two recent cases, however, raised an important related issue. In *Agins v. City of Tiburon* and *San Diego Gas & Electric Co. v. City of San Diego*, property owners claimed that they were entitled to damages for losses incurred when allegedly invalid regulations were applied to their property. Although both these cases reached the Supreme Court, the Court did not resolve the damages issue. Thus, the question remains: What relief is to be awarded after a regulation is found to be unconstitutionally restrictive?

U.S. Department of Agriculture. <u>Perspectives on Prime Land: Background Papers for Seminar on Retention of Prime Lands.</u> Sponsored by the U.S. Department of Agriculture Committee on Land Use, Washington, D.C., July 16-17, 1975. Washington, D.C.: U.S. Department of Agriculture, 1975. 257pp.

The Department of Agriculture Committee on Planning and Policy for Land Use and Land Conservation was established in 1973 to improve coordination among USDA agencies that deal with land use, and to study land use policy issues of concern to agriculture and rural America. In 1975, the committee convened a symposium "to provide the Department with background information necessary for consideration of national policy objectives regarding prime production lands." Papers and review comments were prepared by participants representing universities, public and private agencies, and organizations. The major concern of the symposium was the preservation of prime land--including land to produce timber--to meet future needs. Two papers focused primarily on lands for timber production: "Future Needs for Land to Produce Timber," by John A. Zivnuska and Henry Vaux; and "Demands on Agriculture and Forestry Lands to Serve Complementary Uses," by Raleigh Barlowe.

In their paper, Zivnuska and Vaux conclude that only about one-third of the nation's 500 million acres of commercial forest land is of sufficient quality and held by owners interested in timber production to be "realistically considered as the base for moderately intensive timber management." They add that "policies should be developed that enable and encourage owners of biologically prime forest land to carry out effective forest management on an economic basis."

In his paper, Barlowe concludes that "most of the pressure on productive forest lands will come at sites away from cities that boast special amenity attractions for outdoor recreation. The breaking up of productive forests into small holdings, the influx of second home developments, and the influx of recreational developments poses a threat to the future commercial production potential of many forests."

After the seminar, the USDA Land Use Committee identified a number of recommendations that evolved from the symposium. The Committee urged that the land inventory program authorized by the Rural Development Act be fully implemented in order to provide reliable data on the extent, location, and condition of prime lands, and that programs be developed to educate the public about the need for prime land preservation. The committee also recommended that USDA take the lead in establishing a Land Resources Council, similar to the Water Resources Council, to coordinate land resources programs of the federal government.

American Society of Planning Officials. *Subdividing Rural America: Impacts of Recreational Lot and Second Home Development*. Prepared for the Council of Environmental Quality; Department of Housing and Urban Development, Office of Policy Development and Research; and Appalachian Regional Commission. Washington, D.C.: U.S. Government Printing Office, 1976. 139pp.

This book focuses on the economic, environmental, and social impacts of recreational and second home developments throughout the United States. Sponsored jointly by the Council on Environmental Quality, the Department of Housing and Urban Development, and the Appalachian Regional Commission, the study was carried out at the height of the recreational land sales boom of the early 1970's, just prior to the energy crisis and economic recession of 1974. Its purpose was to provide an accurate source of information on the extent of recreational land development, where it is occurring, and its present and potential effects on our landscape, economy, and society. The authors were also charged with making recommendations for solving some of the problems caused by this development. Accomplished with the assistance of The Urban Land Institute, The Conservation Foundation, and Richard L. Ragatz Associates, Inc., the study provided the first comprehensive national picture of second home development.

According to the report, some benefits, such as economic stimulation in some rural areas, have resulted from recreational land development. However, the study concludes that the potential for substantial negative impact is great. The 10,000,000 recreational lots catalogued in the study had contributed to such environmental problems as surface water pollution and erosion. Economically, they caused strain on local governments in providing services. Socially, they contributed to changes in the composition and character of rural societies. The authors attribute these problems to lack of adequate regulation and control, and warn that, despite the decline in recreational land development at the time of the book's publication, the trend is likely to pick up again in the future. They recommend that federal, state, and local governments (with local jurisdictions bearing the major responsibility) modify existing regulations or implement new ones to provide for better evaluation of sites proposed for development, to determine facility needs and costs, and to protect buyers adequately.

Keene, John C., et.al. *Untaxing Open Space - An Evaluation of the Effectiveness of Differential Assessment of Farms and Open Space.* Prepared by the Regional Science Research Institute in Philadelphia for the Council on Environmental Quality. Washington, D.C.: U.S. Government Printing Office, 1976. 401pp.

Prepared by the Regional Science Research Institute in Philadelphia under contract to the Council on Environmental Quality, this study evaluates the effectiveness of differential assessment of farmland in achieving two objectives: (1) reducing the tax burden of farmers and owners of undeveloped land; and (2) preserving open spaces in rural areas. Part One of the report summarizes differential assessment laws of the 42 states which at that time had adopted them, and discusses the general effectiveness of differential assessment. Part Two presents nine detailed case studies, a statistical analysis of supply and demand in the land market, and an extensive bibliography.

Analysis is restricted to agricultural lands in general and to differential assessment laws falling under three classifications: preferential assessment, deferred taxation, and restrictive agreements. Specific forest and timber taxation programs are not covered, although the open-space tax programs of 17 states include forest and timber land in the definition of agricultural lands.

Under pure preferential assessment, eligible open-space land is assessed at its farm value rather than at market value. Deferred taxation programs impose the requirement that owners who convert their land to non-eligible uses pay some or all of the taxes from which they were excused under differential assessment. Restrictive agreements require owners to sign written contracts governing conditions under which land may be converted.

The study concludes that "differential assessment is a generally effective means for conferring tax benefits on participating landowners." However, not all differential assessment programs are equally successful. The study finds that deferred taxation penalties and restrictive agreements act as deterrents to landowner participation. Consequently, the authors recommend that states adopt pure preferential assessment laws with few eligibility conditions and a minimum of "red tape."

Regarding the second objective of differential assessment laws--preservation of open spaces--the study concludes: "Except for a few specific situations, which account for a small fraction of potential sales of farmland, differential assessment is not likely to be effective in achieving land use objectives." In fact, the authors assert that differential assessment programs are actually "counterproductive in terms of the broader goals of urban development" unless they are part of a larger, comprehensive land use regulation system. They favor government regulation as a means to achieve land use objectives and recommend that differential assessment laws be combined with comprehensive land development and conservation regulations.

Healy, Robert G., and Rosenberg, John S. <u>Land Use and the States</u>. 2d ed. Baltimore: The Johns Hopkins University Press for Resources for the Future, 1979. 284pp.

In <u>Land Use and the States</u>, Healy and Rosenberg describe and analyze the increased direct involvement, beginning in the late 1960's, of state governments in controlling land use. Although land use had traditionally been a subject left to local authorities, the increasing scale of development projects and public concern about environmental, aesthetic, and social impacts led such states as California, Florida, Hawaii, Oregon, and Vermont to pass laws requiring state approval of certain types of projects. Typically, such laws governed only large scale developments ("developments of regional impact") or those located in sensitive areas ("areas of critical concern"). For example, Vermont's Act 250 (1970) governed only development projects with more than ten lots, while California's land use legislation regulated construction along the state's scenic and ecologically sensitive coastline.

The authors present a history of the state land use control movement, a rationale for state involvement, and detailed case studies of state activity in Vermont, California, and Florida. They also describe alternative methods of state involvement (from project-by-project review to formal land use planning) and discuss political, administrative, and economic side effects. Instead of either complete localism or complete centralization, "power over land use should be lodged with the level of government appropriate to the problem," the authors argue. They also believe that "land use controls need not--and probably should not--await the development of comprehensive plans," asserting that the very process of regulation results in more realistic plans. Finally, the authors propose a "menu" of possibilities for state involvement in land use control. The element adopted will vary with the individual conditions and problems of each state, but at minimum will involve mandatory local planning and land regulation and state review of local decisions affecting important non-local interests.

II: Forest Land Use Issues and Policy

A surging public demand for timber during the 1970's, combined with controversy over timber harvesting practices on the National Forests and growing interest in non-commodity values and uses of the forests, stimulated examination of United States forest policy generally. While many studies focused on the role of the National Forests, investigators also looked at policies to encourage timber production on non-federal woodlands. Facilitated by the Forest and Rangeland Renewable Resources Planning Act of 1974, there appeared to be a growing interest in the development of comprehensive policies that considered all three major forest land owners--the federal government, the timber industry, and small private woodland owners. The reports reviewed in this section consider the roles of these sectors generally, as well as the allocation of forest land to the various resource uses. One Third of the Nation's Land, the report of the Public Land Law Review Commission, focused on the federal lands, their roles and management direction. Symposia by Resources for the Future and others looked at forest policy broadly, as well as the institutions that influence it. Marion Clawson examined issues in forest land use allocation. In The Yankee Forest, the Yale School of Forestry provided a regional strategy for forest policy development in New England. Finally, in the belief that to fully understand current issues one has to know how we got where we are, we have included a history, Forest and Range Policy: Its Development in the United States, a 1980 revision of Samuel Trask Dana's classic 1956 work.

Public Land Law Review Commission. One Third of the Nation's Land: A Report to the President and to the Congress by the Public Land Law Review Commission. Washington, D.C.: U.S. Government Printing Office, 1970. 342pp.

Established by Act of Congress in 1964, the Commission was charged with conducting a comprehensive study of 724.4 million acres of federally owned public lands, including a review of statutes, policies, and practices of the federal land management agencies; compilation of data on public demands on the lands' resources; and the submission of recommendations for changes in existing laws, regulations, and policies for the public lands. While all the federal lands technically fell within the Commission's purview, its work had the greatest impact on policy for the public domain managed by the Bureau of Land Management and the National Forests.

In its report, the Commission first advanced the basic principle that the historic policy of large-scale disposal of the public lands "...be revised and that future disposals should be of only those lands that will achieve maximum benefit for the general public in non-federal ownership, while retaining in federal ownership those whose values must be preserved so they may be enjoyed and used by all Americans."

Another basic principle involved a theory of dominant use. While plans for use and management of the public lands should consider "all possible uses and the maximum number of compatible uses should be permitted," the Commission said that "where a unit within an area managed for many uses can contribute a maximum benefit through one particular use, that should be recognized as the dominant use, and the land should be managed to avoid interference with fulfillment of such dominant use."

The Commission went on to advance 137 numbered recommendations. Some of the more significant for forest land use and forest policy-making:

- "All public land agencies should be required to formulate long-range, comprehensive land use plans for each state or region, relating such plans not only to internal agency programs but also to land use plans and attendant management programs of other agencies."

- "State and local governments should be given an effective role in Federal agency planning; Federal land use plans should be developed in consultation with these governments, circulated to them for comments, and should conform to state or local zoning to the maximum extent feasible..."

- "Existing research programs related to the public lands should be expanded for greater emphasis on environmental quality."

- "Congress should authorize and require the public land agencies to condition the granting of rights or privileges to the public land or their resources on compliance with applicable environmental control measures governing operations off public land which are closely related to the rights or privileges granted."

- "There should be statutory requirement that those public lands that are highly productive for timber be classified for commercial timber production as the dominant use..."

- "Dominant timber production units should be managed primarily on the basis of economic factors so as to maximize net returns to the federal treasury."

- "Communities and firms dependent on public land timber should be given consideration in the management and disposal of public land timber."

- "Controls to assure that timber harvesting is conducted so as to minimize adverse impacts on the environment on and off the public lands must be imposed."

A number of the Commission's recommendations were incorporated in the Federal Land Policy and Management Act (The Bureau of Land Management's "Organic Act") in 1976 (P.L. 94-579), with particular application to the public domain managed by BLM. In particular, that Act reversed the national policy of disposal of the public domain and required that it be managed under principles of sustained-yield and multiple-use. The Commission's recommendations for planning for the public lands were incorporated into that Act and subsequent acts applicable to the USDA Forest Service, particularly the National Forest Management Act of 1976 (P.L. 94-558). Both the BLM and the Forest Service statutes incorporated requirements for a stronger voice in federal lands decision-making by local and state governments. However, the dominant-use recommendations were not included in either act.

Clawson, Marion, ed. <u>Forest Policy for the Future: Conflict, Compromise, Consensus</u>. Papers and discussions from a Forum on Forest Policy for the Future, May 8-9, 1974, Washington, D.C. RFF Working Paper LW-1. Baltimore: Johns Hopkins University Press for Resources for the Future, 1974. 360pp.

With controversy building over clearcutting on the National Forests and the timber industry pressing for increased timber harvest to meet demonstrable demands for lumber and fiber, Resources for the Future in 1974 convened a symposium which Marion Clawson told participants was "conceived of as a step in the direction of formulating forest policy for the nation." The forum focused on four background papers: "Future Demand for U.S. Forest Resources," by Leonard L. Fischman; "Conflicts, Strategies and Possibilities for Consensus in Forest Land Use and Management," by Marion Clawson; "Forestry Investments for Multiple Use Among Multiple Ownership Types," by John A. Zivnuska; and "A Search for Consensus," by Joseph L. Fisher. A team of rapporteurs summarized the discussion and their notes were included in these papers. About 200 persons, broadly representative of forest interest groups, attended.

In his paper Clawson suggests that conflict among the many uses of American forests might be lessened if timber management on the most productive forest land were intensified. He postulates a "compatibility matrix," which identifies the degree of compatibility between various uses, as a more precise management tool than the accepted classification of "multiple use," "dominant," or "single" use.

In a final summary presentation at the forum, William E. Towell, then president of the American Forestry Association, saw these potential areas of agreement:

- the need for long-term forestry programs with assured levels of funding;

- increased emphasis on non-industrial private forest lands;

- reforestation of productive forest land in need of planting;

- increased forestry research;

- better utilization of forest products;

- better protection of forests from disease and wildfire;

- improved program in forest education for land managers and landowners; and

- greater attention to forest land amenities.

He identified five areas of continuing conflict: how much wilderness is needed and where; the question of limiting log exports; the future of clearcutting; the pace of conversion of old-growth stands to vigorous young stands on the National Forests of the Pacific Northwest; and the Environmental Impact Statement, which he said some participants felt was being used as a political tool to block timber harvest on the National Forests.

No specific recommendations resulted from the forum, but there was support for the creation (recommended by the President's Advisory Panel on Timber and the Environment) of a permanent national board or council on forest policy to carry on a continuing review of forest policy.

Clawson, Marion. _Forests For Whom and For What?_ Baltimore: Johns Hopkins University Press for Resources for the Future, 1975. 175pp.

In this volume for the "non-specialist," Clawson discusses seven "pressing" forest policy issues: how much land to devote to forests; how much forest land to withdraw from harvest; how to harvest timber; National Forest management; output from small private forests; timber needs and environmental constraints; and export of forest products. He then proceeds to construct a framework for analysis based on five factors: physical and biological feasibility and consequences; economic efficiency;

economic welfare or equity; social or cultural acceptability; and operational or administrative practicality. Succeeding chapters discuss each of these factors.

In a final chapter, Clawson presents some conclusions on the seven issues.

On the preservation of forest land, Clawson advises, "Expend no efforts in preserving forested land." He continues: "The acreages of forest land likely to be diverted from forestry to non-forestry uses are small compared with the total forest area. The need for forest land is not so acute as to require the preservation in forests of all land capable of growing commercial trees." Clawson argues for more intensive production from better sites, but does suggest that society control some uses of presently forested land, specifically citing second home developments.

On withdrawals of land from timber harvest, Clawson concludes that "The amount and location of commercial forest land to withdraw from all timber harvests depends upon the purpose of the withdrawal, the productivity site classification of the land, its ownership, and whether the land is now covered with merchantable timber or whether the tree cover must be restored." He believes "productivity site classification is perhaps the most important factor of all in considering which lands to withdraw." He suggests a generous withdrawal of publicly owned forest land in low-site classes tempered by the amount of low-site land relative to land of high productivity in the region. In the Pacific Northwest, he says, one could withdraw most of the less productive sites; in the Black Hills, where overall site productivity is low, "One would have little forest land left for harvest if all the lower productive sites were withdrawn..."

Clawson admits to ambivalence in dealing with non-industrial private forests. He advances a thesis explored in detail in some of his later work, asking, "Is their accomplishment really so bad given the circumstances under which they must operate? NIPF owners may be poor foresters but good forest economists." He suggests that "if culturally and politically accepted, public assistance be limited to better sites, larger ownerships, in areas where there is a market for the wood grown."

Haney, Harry L., and Gunter, John E., eds. <u>Proceedings of the Forest Taxation Symposium (November 30-December 1, 1977, Blacksburg, Virginia)</u>. Sponsored by Virginia Polytechnic Institute and State University, School of Forestry and Wildlife Resources and Cooperative Extension Service; and the U.S. Department of Agriculture, Forest Service, State and Private Forestry; in cooperation with the Society of American Foresters. Publication FWS 2-78. Blacksburg, VA.: Virginia Polytechnic Institute and State University, Cooperative Extension Service, 1978. 197pp.

This symposium was intended to "...present the latest information available on the economic, administrative, political, and resource allocation aspects of forest tax policy" to managers in industry, government, and professional associations concerned with forest taxation. No particular tax policies or reforms were advocated.

Symposium presentations set forth the pros and cons of various types of taxation, including property taxes (using land, standing timber, and site productivity as the base), yield taxes, and income taxes. Congressional, industry, landowner, and federal agency (including IRS) perspectives were presented. The specific experiences of various states in moving from ad valorem to modified assessment laws, and from ad valorem to yield tax laws also were discussed. Case studies of New York, Georgia, Florida, Washington, Michigan, and California were used to address issues.

In his paper entitled "Impact of Tax Reform on Timber Taxation," attorney Meade Whitaker concludes that forestry has not been adversely affected by federal tax law changes over the years, even with the passage of the 1976 Tax Reform Act. Complexity has been a problem of overriding concern, but simplification is unlikely in the future, he says.

On the state level, various alternative approaches to timber taxation have been tried with varying degrees of success. John H. Stock, Commissioner of the Adirondack Park Agency, pointed out that the New York State legislature failed in several attempts to modify the property tax system to favor timber land. In California, however, a yield tax similar to that enacted earlier in Washington was substituted for a modified property tax with considerable success in terms of revenue generated, improved forest management, and extent of public support, according to William McKillop, Professor of Forest Economics, University of California, Berkeley.

In a symposium wrap-up entitled "Where Do We Go From Here?" Robert S. Manthy, professor of Forest Economics at Michigan State University, questions two assumptions implicit in many of the panelists' remarks--that intensive management of non-industrial forest land is needed to meet future timber requirements and that the form of forest land taxes determines management intensity. He suggests additional research into the impacts, particularly the long-term conservation impacts, of alternative forms of taxation. He also suggests that more attention be given to the size and timing of taxes (as opposed to the form) and to the use of taxation to achieve non-timber and other social objectives.

Convery, Frank J., and Ralston, Charles W., eds. <u>Forestry and Long Range Planning</u>. Durham, N.C.: Duke University School of Forestry and Environmental Studies, 1977. 227pp.

   This collection of papers analyzes the historical and political context of forestry planning and the uses and limitations of certain planning techniques, providing an overview of how forest planning is carried out in both the public and private sectors.

   The first section traces the history of forest planning from its beginnings in Northern Europe to the current problems faced by the Forest Service in implementing the Multiple Use Sustained Yield Act. Subsequent sections cover analytic methods and quantitative techniques in planning, from commodity projection to cost-benefit analysis and linear programming. Industry's approach to long range planning is treated from the national perspective and that of a particular corporation, Westvaco.

   In an epilogue, the editors present a list of "guidelines" for forest planners. Some of the most trenchant:

- the political dimensions of the planning process should be faced squarely;

- beware of the model or computer program touted as the solution to your problems--skepticism should grow as the complexity of the model increases;

- whenever a planning alternative calls for the restriction of individual freedom, a respect for human autonomy should guide the planner to choose that means of restriction which is the least confining;

- a sense of vision is important, but it is also important that alternative and perhaps contradictory visions be encouraged to co-exist; the future is by definition so uncertain that instead of emphasizing the accommodation of projected requirements, forest planning strategy might better be oriented towards minimizing the risk of large social losses, at least at the macro level.

This is perhaps the most comprehensive (and literate) treatment available on contemporary forest planning, covering the historical development of forest planning, planning in the context of policy issues in the 1970's, and some technical aspects of forest planning.

Convery, Frank J., and Davis, Jean E., eds. <u>Centers of Influence and U.S. Forest Policy</u>. Durham, N.C.: Duke University School of Forestry and Environmental Studies, 1977. 166pp.

    This book presents a collection of papers prepared for a 1977 Duke University symposium on the people and institutions that affect forest policy. The selections focus on six "centers of influence" in the policy process: the White House and Office of Management and Budget (OMB), the judiciary, the bureaucracy, the Congress, interest groups, and the press.

    The symposium was intended to provide an understanding of how each center approaches the policy process and to suggest ways policymaking could be improved. Special attention was given to economic perspectives in the policy process.

    In separate sections of the book, each center of influence is analyzed by three or four authors (symposium panelists), at least one of whom provides an "outsider's view." The relation of each sphere to the policy process as a whole is described in detail. In an overview chapter, the editors point to a lack of "a focal point in the system that will give <u>sustained</u> attention to the spectrum of forest policy issues involved in an <u>integrated</u> fashion." The editors look to the Executive Branch--particularly the President, the Secretary of Agriculture, and OMB--for sustained, integrated leadership.

Reidel, Carl H. <u>The Yankee Forest: A Prospectus</u>. A Report of the Yale School of Forestry and Environmental Studies, Fifth Forest Project. New Haven: Yale University, 1978. 31pp.

    In an address to the New England Section of the Society of American Foresters in 1976, Charles H. W. Foster, Dean of the Yale University School of Forestry and Environmental Studies, called for a regional strategy for development of New England's forests. This report examines the feasibility of such a regional strategy. Reidel contends that if coordinated regional action in forest management is not achieved, the forest lands which cover 80 percent of New England will continue to be underutilized or, worse, carelessly exploited.

    The author highlights the dominant ecological and economic characteristics of New England forests and calls for a comprehensive program of multiple-use management primarily based in state and local planning, but also solidly reflective of regional interdependencies and linkages. Reidel sees three major obstacles to development of a region-wide strategy: (1) lack of data appropriate to regional analyses; (2) poor institutional coordination among forestry agencies, both public and private; and (3) a public (including woodland owners) that is not well informed about forest management and policy needs. Among the report's recommendations:

- Forest Service and State Forest Surveys should be updated and schedules sychronized;

- university-based research should be coordinated and a Harvard-Yale joint center for forest studies created;

- a regional New England Forest Information Center should be established;

- the region's institutional capacity should be strengthened through establishment of state forest policy commissions and a regional forestry commission, designation of New England as a separate area for Forest Service planning, and allocation of a major forest planning role to the New England River Basins Commission;

- a program of organizational research should be developed, including examination of such issues as intergovernmental relations, tax programs and incentives, and effectiveness of landowner cooperatives;

- a comprehensive program of public information should be initiated, including films, videotapes, articles, regional conferences, and continuing education for forestry professionals.

As a regional forest development strategy, the Yankee Forest concept could serve as a prototype for other areas of the nation.

Fairfax, Sally K., and Dana, Samuel Trask. <u>Forest and Range Policy: Its Development in the United States</u>. 2d ed. New York: McGraw-Hill Book Company, 1980. 458pp.

In considering forest policy and forest land use issues, it is useful--indeed essential--that we understand how we got where we are. This book, an extensive revision of Dana's 1956 classic, is perhaps the best work available that tracks forest and range issues from the King's Broad Arrow policy of Colonial times through enactment of the National Forest Management Act and the Federal Land Policy and Management Act in 1976.

The book is comprehensive, covering the early history of the public domain; the establishment of National Forests and National Parks during the "Golden Era" of Gifford Pinchot and Theodore Roosevelt; the development of the forests and parks by the CCC during the Depression; the growth of wildland recreation following WWII; the emergence of controversy over clearcutting in the 1960's and the rise of the environmental movement which culminated in the array of pollution control and environmental protection laws of the 1970's; the development of the Forest and

Rangeland Renewable Resources Planning Act of 1964; and, finally, the controversy and compromise that resulted in the National Forest Management Act.

This is not a book exclusively about National Forests and the Forest Service; it also covers in some depth the Bureau of Land Management, the National Park Service, the Soil Conservation Service, state forestry laws, and other agencies, organizations, and statutes which affect forest and range management. The book perceptively analyzes interactions between the agencies, statutes, public opinion, and management technology over time and explains why the public land systems are as they are, how the federal land management agencies evolved, and identifies the central thrusts of past policy that still endure.

Central themes of resource policy of particular interest are the early conflicts between concepts of preservation versus utilization, the persistent conflicts between the Forest Service and the Park System (which Fairfax sees as healthy competitive tension), recurrent efforts by Secretaries of Interior to annex the Forest Service and National Forest System, the long campaign to impose management on the public range and the struggle of BLM to emerge from "enduring obscurity," Pinchot's tenacious efforts in forest land management, and the development of the concept of sustained yield forestry. Fairfax wields a very sharp pen, which she uses to prick virtually every forest and range interest group.

III: Forest Products Supply and Demand

What is the situation with regard to the supply of and demand for forest resources? The reports reviewed in this section deal with estimates of future supply and demand, some of the factors that affect them, and ways in which supplies of forest goods and services might be increased. The President's Advisory Panel on Timber and the Environment looked at ways in which timber supplies could be increased while protecting the environment. A National Academy of Sciences study committee examined the nation's use of materials, including wood, and the environmental effects of materials use. Forest economist Lloyd Irland sought to answer the fundamental question "Is timber scarce?" The next two reports are the most recent Forest Service assessments of forest and rangeland productive capability, and future demand. The first looks at all forest and range resources; the other focuses on timber. Opportunities to increase supplies also are identified. The final report presents the forest products industry's findings on opportunities to increase timber production in 25 key states.

President's Advisory Panel on Timber and the Environment. <u>Final Report</u>. Washington, D.C.: U.S. Government Printing Office, 1973. 541 pp.

A five-member panel was appointed by President Nixon in 1971 to "advise the President on matters associated with increasing the nation's supply of timber to meet growing housing needs while protecting and enhancing the quality of our environment." The report of the panel "considers the entire forest resources of the United States, public and private, and their contribution to national well-being," and the role of U.S. forests in the world forest economy.

The central policy issue for meeting wood needs for the 1970's and 1980's, according to the panel, is "at what rate should old growth inventory on the national forests be converted to well-managed new stands to meet both current and future timber needs?" The panel recommended that "national forest timber sales be brought up to and maintained at allowable harvest levels on all forests where there is sufficient volume of market demand." It disavowed strict evenflow on old-growth forests (the harvest of no more timber within a time period than is grown), "contingent on adequate provisions for financing whatever intensified timber management is needed to support the higher rate of cutting."

Among the panel's major recommendations:

- Federal agencies should prepare a comprehensive nationwide program of forest development and timber supply to the year 2020;

- Commercial forest lands not withdrawn for wilderness or other specific uses should be designated for commercial timber production and other compatible uses and managed in accordance with other national policies;

- Harvesting of old growth should be accelerated; the report says that data indicate "possibilities for increasing the old growth cutting rate in the range of 50-100 percent";

- There should be a complementary program of intensified management to support the increased harvest levels, including prompt regeneration;

- The federal government should maintain incentive programs to encourage private landowners to protect the environment of their forest lands and increase timber production;

- For recreation uses of public forests, fees should be established which are "administratively feasible, equitable, and reflect the value of the recreational opportunity and cost of providing the area and facilities."

The panel was an articulate proponent of relaxing the Forest Service's policy of nondeclining evenflow and accelerating the pace at which the old growth forests of the Pacific Northwest are converted to fast-growing young stands. While a direct relationship with the PAPTE recommendation is impossible to establish, the National Forest Management Act of 1976 did provide for departure from nondeclining evenflow under limited conditions. The report's recommendation that commercial forest land not withdrawn for wilderness be designated for timber production is paralleled in the current debate over "release" language in legislation designating wilderness as a result of the Forest Service's RARE II (Roadless Area Review and Evaluation). Further, the panel's recommendation for comprehensive, long-term forest planning may have helped set the stage for subsequent development of the Forest and Rangeland Renewable Resources Planning Act of 1974 (RPA).

National Academy of Sciences/National Academy of Engineering. *Man, Materials and Environment.* A Report to the National Commission on Materials Policy by the Study Committee on Environmental Aspects of a National Materials Policy. Cambridge: The MIT Press, 1973. 236pp.

    The Resource Recovery Act of 1970 required the formation of a National Commission on Materials Policy to recommend a comprehensive national policy for materials usage. For the Commission, the Study Committee on Environmental Aspects of a National Materials Policy examined ways in which environmental safeguards could be incorporated into the nation's use of materials. The Committee said that environmental impacts should be considered in every public and private decision regarding materials usage and called for national goals for materials consumption. It recommended a series of incentives and administrative action to reduce waste and facilitate improved utilization with appropriate environmental safeguards. Foreseeing an increase in the future demand for materials, resulting in environmental stress, the Committee also called for a major program of research into all aspects of environmental deterioration. Regarding timber, the Committee found that while there was considerable knowledge of the environmental impacts of forest management, more effort was needed to apply basic research to management problems. The Committee also recommended research into environmentally efficient uses of forest products, particularly the use of forest residue for energy.

Irland, Lloyd C. *Is Timber Scarce? The Economics of a Renewable Resource.* Yale University School of Forestry and Environmental Studies Bulletin No. 83. New Haven: Yale University, 1974. 97pp.

    Irland's avowed purpose was to improve "the basis for __diagnosis__ of natural resource supply conditions" (emphasis his). His economic analysis tested the hypothesis "The United States has experienced steadily increasing timber scarcity and faces increasingly severe scarcities in the future." Irland confined his study to welfare impacts on the consumer under conditions of resource scarcity, which he defined as "a social problem resulting from a rising real price of natural resource products, within a specified framework of time and place."

    Drawing on measures used by Barnett and Morse and Ruttan and Callahan (real price), and Vanek (net trade balance), he chose as his main indicators of economic scarcity an upward trend of real prices for timber and a downward trend in the net foreign trade balance in timber. Irland found that during the period 1950-70, the real price of timber products declined and the net balance of foreign trade improved. Thus, he rejected the scarcity hypothesis. Factors such as the resurgence of second growth forests, regrowth of farmland into forest, and benefits of wildfire and pest control were responsible in large part for the increased availability of wood, Irland said, though acknowledging that "these gains were temporary and will not recur." However, Irland saw long-run forces that were cause for optimism, including opportunities for increased investments on public and private forest land, rising yields from managed plantations, and the benefits of technology.

Irland observed that "the worst predictions of prospective forest depletion" were based on the assumption that per capita consumption of paper products would continually increase. He then questioned whether stable per capita consumption of paper products translates into a social welfare loss. He concluded that it should be possible to manage demand as well as supply and suggested that ways be found to curtail "low priority" uses of timber. This, he said "is ultimately the only way out of the trap of ever rising consumption versus finite resources."

U.S. Department of Agriculture, Forest Service. <u>An Assessment of the Forest and Rangeland Situation in the United States.</u> Washington, D.C.: U.S. Government Printing Office, 1980. 631pp.

The Forest and Rangeland Renewable Resources Planning Act of 1974 requires a comprehensive assessment of all the nation's forest and rangeland resources, the demands anticipated over the next 40 years, and opportunities to increase production. The first Assessment was issued in 1976; this is the second. (The next is required in 1990.)

The Assessment looks at the nation's 1.7 billion acres of forest and rangelands in all ownerships. Specifically, it looks at forest and rangelands, outdoor recreation and wilderness, wildlife and fish, range, timber (see following report review), and water.

The Assessment begins with three basic assumptions: (1) that the population will grow to 300 million by 2030, even though the rate of growth will decline; (2) the gross national product will increase in the same period 3.7 times, to $5,160 billion; and (3) average per capita personal income will rise to $12,020, 2.7 times that of today.

The Assessment subsequently finds that "consumption of forest and range products has been rising rapidly," and "projections show demands for forest and range products rising faster than supplies." On the plus side, the nation has a huge forest and rangeland and water base, 1.7 billion acres or 71 percent of the nation's area, "which can be used to meet demands for nearly all products." The bulk of this forest and range land is privately owned (832 million acres or 53 percent, including relatively small state, county, and municipal lands).

The Assessment concludes that production on the nation's forest and rangelands is below potential; commercial timberland (land not withdrawn from timber production and capable of producing at least 20 cubic feet per acre of industrial wood per year) is producing at three-fifths of capability and rangeland at just over one-third of biological potential. While there presently is no way of quantifying recreation capacity, these lands can supply recreational opportunities "far in excess of foreseeable increases in demand." Likewise, these lands can support a greater diversity and greater numbers of wildlife species. Water yield can also be increased by intensive management.

While opportunities exist to increase production sufficiently to meet projected demands for nearly all resources, "achieving this potential will require more intensive management of much of the land and water base, the integration of all renewable resources in management plans, construction of new facilities, improvements in the efficiency of utilization, and the preservation of some renewable resources." While this will require substantial public and private investments, the Assessment says, they "promise to be profitable."

Several general opportunities are worth noting. First, according to the Assessment, supplies from privately owned lands, particularly small ownerships, can be increased, by cost-sharing programs to finance management, provision of technical assistance, and by landowner educational programs. Second, increases in supplies generally can be facilitated by increased research to develop new technology.

A section of the Assessment deals with "multiple resource interaction"--the effect that management practices to increase supplies of one resource have on the land's capability to supply other resources. To fully evaluate the productive capacity of a tract of land, it may be necessary to understand the interactions among several resources. Some resource uses may be complementary; others are competitive. Wise management decisions require careful evaluation of these interactions.

The Assessment also discusses scientific data and research needs. It recommends that resource surveys be accelerated; there is an average 12-year interval between state timber surveys, according to the Assessment, but in areas of rapid change "inventory cycles of more than five years are of limited usefulness in guiding resource planning and management." The survey should also provide more precise local data. Surveys of use of forest and range products should be improved, as should techniques for collecting data needed for forest management--particularly for non-timber resources--and estimating the cost of different management practices.

The Assessment is the primary document used in the development of the Program, a long-range plan for Forest Service activities which is updated every five years. State forestry agencies contribute data to the Assessment and also use it in the development of their own state programs. Industry sources indicate that it is used as a national and regional data source, but that its information must be augmented by more precise local and regional information collected to meet specific company requirements.

U.S. Department of Agriculture, Forest Service. <u>Analysis of the Timber Situation in the United States, 1952-2030--Review Draft</u>. Washington, D.C.: U.S. Government Printing Office, 1980. 541pp. plus appendices.

This volume, released in the spring of 1980, provides the most comprehensive and current analysis of present timber supplies, capability, anticipated demand, and opportunities to increase supplies. The timber data in the Assessment (see previous report review) were drawn from this volume. It replaces the 1974 publication <u>The Outlook for Timber in the United States</u> as the standard source of national timber data.

The Analysis uses the same demographic and economic assumptions as the Assessment. It amplifies information on demand, supplies, and opportunities.

Projections show demand for most timber products rising rapidly, with a middle-level projection of demand for all wood products to reach 22.7 billion cubic feet in 2000 and 28.3 billion cubic feet in 2030 (compared to 1978 consumption of 13.3 billion cubic feet). Pulpwood will account for about 45 percent of consumption in 2030, compared with one-third today.

Most of the projected growth in demand must be satisfied by domestic forests; improved utilization and increased imports will accommodate only a small portion of anticipated demand. Domestic forests will be called upon to provide 25.1 billion cubic feet by 2030, double the present demand from U.S. forests.

This demand must be met by 483 million acres classed as commercial forest land. Fifty-eight percent (or 278 million acres) of this is in private non-industrial ownership, 14 percent (69 million acres) is owned by industry, and 136 million acres, or 28 percent, is in public ownership, including 89 million acres in National Forests. Most of the timber inventory is in softwoods (456 billion cubic feet). Hardwood growing stock amounts to 255 billion cubic feet.

The timber situation has been improving nationally and in most regions, the Analysis found. Domestic softwood stock increased 11 percent between 1952 and 1977, and hardwoods by 43 percent. The Analysis adds, however, "the increase in inventories has been almost entirely on the young stands in the North and South and chiefly on the farmer and other private ownerships.

Softwood inventories on the forest industry ownerships and the National Forests in the Pacific Coast Section dropped substantially." However, the Analysis concludes that the timber resource in most regions, and particularly in the East, can support larger harvest.

Even so, projected timber demands on domestic forests are rising faster than supplies. If trends continue, there will be "a growing imbalance between the quantity of timber that people would like to consume and the supply." The greatest shortfall will be for softwood timber, with a 3.4 billion cubic feet gap in 2030. According to the Analysis, this will result in a substantial rise in prices for softwood stumpage and products. For hardwoods, however, supplies should be adequate to meet demands for the next two or three decades, after which demand will exceed supply.

If corrective action is not taken, the Analysis warns, the growing economic scarcity of timber "will have significant and adverse effects" on the economy, the environment (as consumers use non-renewable resources requiring processing, with greater uses of energy and greater potential for air and water pollution in extraction and processing) and social well-being. This is not inevitable; there are opportunities to increase supplies. Intensifying management on 168 million acres of commercial timberland, about 35 percent of the total, could result in a net increase in annual timber growth of 12.9 billion cubic feet--an amount about equal to the 1976 timber harvest, according to the Analysis. (However, softwood growth in the South will peak in 2010; the falloff is due to an assumed failure to regenerate stands back to pine after harvest.) Increased utilization and technology for using wood residues in panel products could also extend supply.

Forest Industries Council. <u>Forest Productivity Report</u>.
  Washington, D.C.: National Forest Products Association,
  1980. 66pp.

This report is a summary of 25 state reports, focusing on those states where, in the timber industry's view, the greatest opportunities exist to increase timber production. Overall, more than 400 million acres of commercial forestland on all types of ownerships (public lands, industrial forests, non-industrial private forests) were evaluated. The report identifies these opportunities: in the South, regeneration and intermediate stand management on nonindustrial private forests; in the West, accelerated harvests of old growth forests, especially on public lands, and replacement with vigorous managed stands.

Private non-industrial ownerships, with 60 percent of the commercial forest land studied, have about 57 percent of the opportunities. National Forests, with 15 percent of the land, have 20 percent of the opportunities. Forest industry lands have 17.5 percent of the opportunities on 16 percent of the land.

Capturing all opportunities on 139 million acres of forest land where opportunities were identified would require a current investment of $10.3 billion, the report says. This would increase annual growth by 10.9 billion cubic feet and increase total U.S. net growth by about 50 percent. The report's major recommendations:

- establish a national timber productivity goal that recognizes the long-term growing cycles inherent in forests and is aimed at minimizing real consumer costs and building the potential for an international net trade surplus of forest products.

- establish a favorable economic and socio-political investment climate through tax changes, cost-effective public assistance programs, increased industry support for programs to educate and motivate private woodlands owners, implementation of measures to increase yield and harvests from public forests, and reduced regulation of forest management.

This report is being cited widely in support of changes in tax structure, increased industry attention to efforts aimed at non-industrial forest owners, and increased federal investments in cost-sharing programs and technical assistance. (See report summary of America Grows on Trees: The Promise of Private, Non-Industrial Woodlands, the timber industry's program for increasing timber production from non-industrial private forests, page 47.)

IV: Economic Analysis

While the economics of providing goods and services from forested lands in the various ownerships categories is discussed in a number of the selections covered in this paper, the four selections in this section deal exclusively with methodologies of economic analysis and factors to be considered. Two of them deal with the challenge of arriving at quantitative estimates of outputs, costs and benefits associated with forest "products" (such as wildlife) and services (such as hiking or visual amenities) not sold in the marketplace. Another, by Marion Clawson, addresses factors to be considered in the growing, harvesting, and marketing of timber. The final review is of William F. Hyde's Timber Supply Land Allocation and Economic Efficiency, which constructs an economics efficiency model for timber management.

Krutilla, John V., and Fisher, Anthony C. The Economics of Natural Environments: Studies in the Valuation of Commodity and Amenity Resources. Baltimore: Johns Hopkins University Press for Resources for the Future, 1975. 292pp.

Drawing upon their own previous work and that of other economists, Krutilla and Fisher build a theory to deal with "the valuation of the opportunity costs of activities that can be expressed as loss of amenities otherwise available from a natural environment." The "amenity" values of natural resource sites, say the authors, have traditionally been neglected in reviews of development projects. This study is an early attempt to take them into consideration in standard economic analysis. They describe their work as a "first generation" effort.

Among the amenity values considered by Krutilla and Fisher are demand for outdoor recreation, scientific research opportunities, option value (associated with the irreversibility of a decision to develop), and existence value (derived from the knowledge that a resource exists even if it is not expected to be used in situ by the person assigning value to it). Only one of these, outdoor recreation, is measurable using current econometric techniques (the work of Clawson, Cicchetti and Smith, and others is cited).

Krutilla and Fisher advance a two-point strategy for analyzing resource projects. First, conventional cost-benefit methods are applied, with consideration for environmental costs, but with inclusion of hidden costs (e.g., tax subsidies) to determine the true cost of a project. In many cases, they conclude, development projects cannot be economically justified when all their real costs are revealed. In cases where development still provides for net benefits, the second stage of analysis—evaluation of the benefits of preservation—is conducted. The authors assert that it is not necessary to ascertain exact measurements of all benefits associated with preservation, if some portion of them can be evaluated for the purpose of indicating whether their value would equal or exceed the benefits accrued from development.

The authors apply this analysis to specific cases covering extractive uses versus preservation on public lands (hydropower development in Hells Canyon and molybdenum mining in the White Cloud Peaks); low-intensity versus high-intensity recreational uses (Mineral King Valley); allocation of lands in private ownership to public resource use (prairie wetlands); and the evaluation of alternate approaches to an established development project (Trans-Alaska pipeline).

Krutilla and Fisher conclude by discussing the policy implications of their analysis. They suggest the addition, for planning purposes, of a charge akin to a severance tax to the calculated costs of a development project to represent lost option value and what they term "temporal inconsistency," i.e., changes in demand over time for both the development and the amenity values. Legislative zoning of wilderness areas, with provisions to make rezoning difficult, they add, might insure adequate consideration of the consequences of irreversibility. Finally, the authors urge the creation of independent regional centers to develop the economic methodology for analyzing development projects and for conducting the analysis of contemporary proposals.

The work of Krutilla and Fisher is considered a landmark in the development of methods for analyzing the costs and benefits of developments that involve the irreversible alteration of natural environments.

Clawson, Marion. <u>Decision Making in Timber Production, Harvest and Marketing</u>. Research Paper R-4. Washington, D.C.: Resources for the Future, 1977. 128pp.

Clawson wrote this book "in the conviction that foresters, economists, conservationists, and business interests were not talking in the same terms when they considered the growing and the harvest of timber from particular forest areas."

The report considers the decison-making process in timber management for the small private forest, for the large, vertically integrated forest products company, and for the National Forests. The intent was to focus on the practical problems (particularly when to harvest timber) faced by forest managers or forest landowners.

Clawson discusses three concepts for determining when to harvest: (1) biological relationships of age, growth, and maturity of trees; (2) economic analysis, especially considerations of financial maturity; and (3) production functions, or the relationship of timber growth to "productive inputs" such as land, standing forest, fertilizer, and fire control, interest on capital, and management. He contrasts biological concepts of maturity--specifically the determination of when maxiumum mean annual increment of growth has been reached--with financial maturity.

For the National Forests, Clawson particularly addresses policy for the old-growth forests of the Pacific Northwest and Forest Service concepts of sustained yield (in practice, says Clawson, "that yield which comes from reasonably good 'natural forestry'"), allowable cut (the amount of timber which can be cut annually), and evenflow (cutting no more timber than average annual growth) which, in the case of old-growth, results in annual harvests below the productive potential of a good site. As for fears that there will be a drop-off in available timber when the old growth has been harvested, Clawson says that this can be prevented through intensive management.

Clawson concludes that "there exists a period of years within which the probable exact year of maximum MAI [mean annual increment of growth] or of financial maturity fall, and during which harvest may take place with approximately the same results." However, he points out that there are other factors which affect harvest decisions: the small owner should consider the state of the market and his or her own ownership objectives; the large timber company should consider the cost of processing and effect of harvest decisions on market price. On the National Forests, the Forest Service's interest in maintaining community stability may override economic and biological analysis, Clawson concludes.

Sinden, John A., and Worrell, Albert C. <u>Unpriced Values: Decisions Without Market Prices</u>. New York: John C. Wiley & Sons, 1979. 511pp.

The 1970's saw a significant increase in the use of cost-benefit analysis to assist public policy makers at all levels of government decide among various policy alternatives. In the environment and health areas, however, the application of the science of economic analysis has proved difficult and the subject of controversy because many values associated with health and the environment, such as the health value of clean air or water, or preservation of endangered species, cannot be quantified monetarily. <u>Unpriced Values</u> deals with the problem of placing comparative values on benefits and costs that are not traded in the market, such as scenic beauty, wildlife preservation, gradual change, and human life.

The authors are both forest economists, Sinden at the University of New England, Australia, and Worrell at Yale University. Their book is a technical guidebook for managers, planners, policy analysts, and policy-makers reviewing the strengths and limits of the current methods of cost-benefit analysis for comparing unpriced values with marketplace values.

Part I deals with the concepts surrounding values and valuation, the kinds of value information needed for making decisions, the usefulness of comparative values, and the nature and application of basic economic concepts.

Part II, the largest section of the book, examines the many methods of valuation and analyses currently being used to measure unpriced values by planners, economists, and managers.

The authors group methods into the following categories: rigorous total utility methods, opportunity cost methods, market-price, direct-question methods for estimating monetary value, direct and structural methods for estimating net social benefit, and comparative social value estimations. For each group they discuss specific methodology and then look at examples such as air pollution abatement, maintenance of wildlife, and creating a large park (Gorgelands National Park in Australia) to illustrate the kinds of decisions for which particular methods are suitable. The authors analyze the strengths and weaknesses of each, and compare the results. In general, Sinden and Worrell conclude that "...the concept of net social benefits provides a better idea about the utility and value aspects of policies than any other proposed concept."

Part III discusses why decisions involving unpriced values are considered difficult and shows how appropriate uses of the different methods can overcome difficulties.

The key to making decisions involving unpriced values, according to Sinden and Worrell, is understanding that "different decisions may require different concepts of value and different valuation methods." They urge planners to approach valuation in the context of the particular decision at hand and to define clearly the nature of the decision so that the most appropriate valuation method can be selected. "A clear understanding of the kind of value information needed for the decision will almost make it possible to obtain helpful estimates of comparative values," they assert. Although there is no single, perfect method of valuation, Sinden and Worrell believe that current methods are effective when used in innovative combinations appropriate to particular decision needs.

Hyde, William F. _Timber Supply, Land Allocation, and Economic Efficiency._ Baltimore: The Johns Hopkins University Press for Resources for the Future, 1980. 224pp.

This book discusses the economic efficiency of timber management in both the public and private sectors. Since the Forest Service is the nation's largest single timber manager and producer, much of the discussion is centered around policies and programs for the National Forests. The book's purpose is to "examine how a shift to more efficient timber management would affect [the] controversy" surrounding modern forest management.

Hyde begins by examining the allowable cut timber management model traditionally used by public agencies and some timber companies. He then contrasts it with an "economic efficiency model" and makes short- and long-term projections of timber supply based on economically efficient production techniques. These projections form the basis for his analysis of efficient allocations of land among forest uses. Land allocation decisions are illustrated by two case studies--the Douglas-fir region (the regional level) of the Northwest and the French Pete Creek drainage on the Willamette National Forest in Oregon (the micro level of a single physical unit).

Hyde demonstrates a number of economic ineffeciencies in the allowable cut model and asserts that 4.6 million acres of public land are currently managed inefficiently. His calculations show that harvests from this acreage could be increased by 74 percent; this, he says, would decrease environmental risk over all and increase recreational opportunities on remaining public land. He concludes that if economically efficient management were practiced and prices continued to rise at historical levels, there would be no timber shortfall in the future.

As for the timber industry, Hyde finds that companies have recently begun to move toward efficient silvicultural management, although some companies continue to use variations of the allowable cut model. Hyde then discusses why public agencies have been reluctant to adopt some economic efficiency criteria, and outlines some of the trade-offs involved in a management reorientation. For example, an efficient harvest level which is lower than that set previously might result in unemployment in the community dependent upon the harvest. However, the financial return from efficient management might outweigh the costs of retraining and relocating community residents. Hyde also contends that the laws governing forest management (RPA, NFMA) are not unduly restrictive; rather, "historically reasonable Forest Service administrative policies are today more restrictive than the law," he asserts. Hyde believes it is time for these policies (and their basic assumption of a future timber shortage) to be reevaluated.

Hyde believes "that the expectation of timber shortages is a consequence of simplistic projection methods coupled with outmoded and inefficient timber management practices, and that increasing recreational and environmental demands are more apparent than real constraints on timber production."

V: Management of Forest Resources

This section looks at six reports dealing with management of forest resources. One is a comprehensive text and field guide for forest resource managers. The others look at specific activities and resources: one, prepared by the Environmental Protection Agency in the early 1970's, reviews the then state-of-the-art in control of water pollution from silvicultural activities; another looks at the impacts of a large recreational development in an area containing much forested land; another, at the management of the timber resource to maintain diverse wildlife habitats; another considers wilderness management; and the last, management of eastern hardwoods for multiple benefits.

U.S. Environmental Protection Agency, Office of Air and Water Programs. <u>Methods for Identifying and Evaluating the Nature and Extent of Nonpoint Sources of Pollutants</u>. Washington, D.C.: U.S. Government Printing Office, 1973. 261pp.

In this report, the Environmental Protection Agency attempted to assemble existing knowledge about nonpoint sources of pollutants--their nature and extent, and methods for identifying and evaluating them. Intended as a guide for regional planners and other officials responsible for water quality, the study focuses on four sources of non-point pollutants: agriculture, silviculture, mining, and construction. Each of these areas is described in general terms and the main pollutants and their methods of dispersion are identified and defined. The report then sets forth methods for analyzing pollution from these activities.

While well-managed forests generally do not contribute significantly to water pollution, the report asserts that there is substantial potential for pollution when trees are harvested. Sediment is the major polluter, though organic matter, pesticides, fertilizers, and animal pathogens also may flow from the harvest site. Where tree cover has been removed along streams, thermal pollution may be a problem as well. Among harvesting methods, clearcutting and seed tree are cited as having the highest potential for pollution, because of the amount of vegetation removed and soil exposed. Construction of logging roads also is a major cause of sedimentation, according to this report.

The report acknowledges that "the present state-of-the-art on prediction of pollution from forestlands is very crude." It proceeds to describe methods of predicting the quality and quantity of pollution from a forested watershed, providing data and information sources. This volume, though eight years old, has never been updated.

Duerr, William A.; Teeguarden, Dennis E.; Guttenberg, Sam; and Christiansen, Neils B., eds. <u>Forest Resource Management: Decision-Making Principles and Cases</u>. Two vols. Corvallis, OR: Oregon State University Book Stores, Inc., 1975.

Originally conceived in 1966 as part of an ongoing project to improve professional education in forestry, this two-volume work is both a textbook intended for use primarily by forestry students, and a handbook for resource managers. Its forty-nine chapters cover every conceivable aspect of forest management, with contributors from academia, government, and industry.

The editors strive for a dynamic, non-traditional approach to forestry education, presenting forestry as a system interacting with a larger social setting, and management as decision-making in a social context. They place special emphasis on the total system, stating that "a continuing effort will be made, in the work as an entirety, to convey strongly the sense of holism that is appropriate to forest resource management." Rather than teach students a body of rules for proper forest management, they impart the notion that forestry can be viewed as "sets of resource alternatives" in which all forest uses are taken into account.

Volume I contains four parts: Context, Decision Process, Models in Decision Making, and Services of the Forest. Volume II covers the social environment of forestry and cases in forest resource management. In each volume the authors move from the general to the specific, clarifying their points with case examples and illustrations. The section on decision-making models emphasizes quantitative methods, as the editors felt this subject was lacking in traditional forestry curricula.

Gallatin Canyon Study Team. <u>Impacts of Large Recreational Developments Upon Semi-Primitive Environments: The Gallatin Canyon Synthesis Report</u>. Bozeman, MT: Montana State University, 1976. 141pp.

In the early 1970's, with recreational home developments pushing into remote mountain areas in the West, the Institute of Applied Research at Montana State University, with funding from the National Science Foundation, began a six year study of the environmental and social impacts of the 10,000-acre Big Sky all-season resort in the Gallatin Canyon in southwestern Montana. The purpose of the analysis--by 40 faculty members from 14 disciplines--was to provide an understanding of the impacts of large-scale developments upon semi-primitive environments, and to develop planning and policy guidelines.

The report depicts development as a cyclical process affecting eight "parameters": land use, water quality, air quality, wildlife, recreation, transportation, the economy, and public policy decisions. Big Sky's effects on each of these parameters are analyzed and potential solutions and policy recommendations are set forth.

The study team cautions against a single-issue approach, suggesting that comprehensive land use planning be required as a mechanism for achieving a balanced development strategy. The difficulty of obtaining consensus at the local level tends to create a vacuum in which development proceeds with adverse environmental effects, the study team says; thus federal and state leadership is necessary. Because of the preponderance of National Forest lands in the Gallatin Canyon, the U.S. Forest Service played a key role in Big Sky's development, and better Forest Service planning might have yielded better results, according to the study team.

Effective planning, the report concludes, requires the cooperation of many agencies and hinges on three elements: public participation in the decision-making process prior to development; formulation of a clear set of policies and goals; and the capacity to implement policies through such measures as performance controls and facility siting.

Boyce, Stephen G. <u>Management of Eastern Hardwood Forests for Multiple Benefits (DYNAST-MB)</u>. U.S. Department of Agriculture Forest Service Research Paper SE-168. Asheville, N.C.: U.S. Department of Agriculture, Forest Service, Southeastern Forest Experiment Station, 1977. 116pp.

Passage of the National Forest Management Act of 1976, Boyce points out, "has increased the demand to manage forests for multiple benefits." While foresters are adept at managing forests to optimize individual resources, says Boyce, "our attempts to match an increasing variety of benefits with an increasing variety of management techniques are leading to conflicting actions on the same piece of land." He continues: "How to harmonize management actions to yield a desired combination of multiple benefits is perhaps the most puzzling and intractable problem for forestry in this century."

DYNAST--an acronym for "Dynamically Analytic Silviculture Technique"--is a systems model which permits the manager to "assess an infinite number of management alternatives by predicting how each policy would affect timber production, habitat for a number of animal species, sediment flow, and aesthetics of the landscape."

The report's first section provides a descriptive explanation of how to use the system; the second presents the mathematical equations necessary to convert forest data into quantitative form. The system is based on the relationship between resource benefits and forest habitats, which Boyce classifies according to age classes of trees. In the multiple benefit model, the "hypothetical harvest of timber is regulated to guide the model toward equilibrium of age classes yielding a constant annual flow of harvested timber and other benefits." Equipped with knowledge about the benefits from particular distributions of habitat in the forest, the manager can use the computer model to determine the biologically possible combinations of benefits for the tract under study, and then project the combinations of habitats resulting from different management actions.

Hendee, John C.; Stankey, George H.; and Lucas, Robert C. *Wilderness Management*. Miscellaneous Publication No. 1365. Washington, D.C.: U.S. Department of Agriculture, Forest Service, 1977. 381pp.

Much has been written about the political issues related to Congressional designation of wilderness, very little about the actual management of wilderness after designation. This volume, written by three Forest Service research scientists, with four chapters contributed by other specialists, is intended to start building a literature of wilderness management. "Once the decision has been made to set aside a tract of land as wilderness," the authors write, "the long-term preservation of those values that originally led to wilderness legislation will depend on management." They add: "the management challenge is especially important because of growing pressures on wilderness use and man's indirect impact's on all lands." While technically a Forest Service publication, the book is aimed at all public land managing agencies with wilderness responsibility.

For its time, the volume is comprehensive. Its 16 chapters address six main areas: (1) the setting, principally historical background on the development of the wilderness concept, with two chapters by historian Roderick Nash; (2) the legal basis for wilderness, dealing with the wilderness statutes and the current (as of the writing) and projected status of the wilderness system; (3) management concepts and direction, dealing with a wilderness planning framework and carrying capacity; (4) important elements for management, specifically ecosystems, wildlife and fire; (5) wilderness use and its management, addressing problems of visitor use and ways of managing visitor behavior and protection of the wilderness environment; (6) problems and opportunities, which identifies current "issues and challenges."

The authors advance 11 principals of wilderness management, some obvious, others subtle in their implications. Some of the more salient: "The management of wilderness must be viewed in relationship to the management of adjacent lands." "The purpose of wilderness management is to produce human values and benefits." "Wilderness preservation requires a carrying capacity constraint." "Wilderness management should strive to selectively

-34-

reduce the physical and social-psychological impacts of use" (that is, types of wilderness use should be ranked according to physical-biological impact upon the resource and socio-psychological impacts on other uses, and when restrictions are necessary, those with greatest impact should be the first ones controlled). "The management of individual areas should be governed by a concept of non-degradation."

The final chapter looks at future issues and challenges in wilderness management. A key question relates to controlling impacts from recreational use: How can visitor use be regulated while respecting visitor freedom and ensuring equitable treatment among users?

Thomas, Jack Ward, tech. ed. <u>Wildlife Habitat in Managed Forests - The Blue Mountains of Oregon and Washington</u>. U.S. Department of Agriculture, Forest Service, Agriculture Handbook No. 553. Washington, D.C.: U.S. Government Printing Office, 1979. 512pp.

Not long ago, writes editor Jack Ward Thomas, resource management professionals were secure in the tenet that "good timber management is good wildlife management." But times have changed, and "wildlife managers and foresters alike have found that it is not necessarily so."

This volume looks not at individual species, but at habitats--"the key to organizing knowledge about wildlife so it can be used in forest management." Habitats are classified and described so that they can be considered simultaneously with timber management. Using data from the Blue Mountains of Oregon and Washington, the authors classify the types of wildlife found in different forest habitats--riparian zones, edges, snags, dead and down wood, cliffs--and describe how the timber resource might be managed to preserve or enhance the habitats. In support of their thesis that wildlife and timber management can be compatible, they then offer practical guides on how this dual objective can be accomplished through specific forest land use management techniques. The final chapter describes the methodology for assessing the cost of providing wildlife habitat in terms of wood production foregone.

VI: National Forest Policy

The six reports and studies reviewed in this section deal specifically with policy for management of federally owned forest lands, primarily the National Forests. A 1976 symposium convened by the Society of American Foresters and the American Bar Association examined the situation that existed just prior to passage of the National Forest Mangement Act of 1976; two other reports in this section consider that legislation, one emphasizing economic analysis of management direction. Another study examines policy for the 49 National Forests east of the 100th meridian. Also included is a General Accounting Office study of Forest Service planning, and a report on the relationships between federal resource lands and neighboring communities and landowners.

LeMaster, Dennis C., and Popovich, Luke, eds. Crisis in Federal Forest Land Mangement. Proceedings of a Symposium sponsored by the Forest Resources Committee and Natural Resources Section of the American Bar Association and the Natural Resources Law Working Group of the Society of American Foresters, Denver, Colorado, November 4-5, 1976. Washington, D.C.: Society of American Foresters, 1977. 110pp.

Convened after the Fourth Circuit Court decision on Izaak Walton League v. Butz, the Monongahela National Forest clearcutting suit, this symposium looked at ways of resolving disputes over National Forest management. Participants included academic figures, industrial and environmental spokespersons, and Congressional and federal officials who had key roles in the development of policy. One panel addressed the problems of legislating policy for federal forest lands, another the problems of policy implementation, a third the ascendance of the judiciary in forest policy, while a fourth tentatively offered some suggestions.

The "crisis," it was agreed, was due to increasing relative scarcity of forest resources and inadequate policy direction by Congress. Solutions were judged to be premature until the National Forest Management Act was fully implemented and Congress had exercised its oversight responsibilities for the Forest and Rangeland Renewable Resources Planning Act of 1974 (RPA).

D. Michael Harvey, Chief Counsel, Senate Committee on Energy and Natural Resources, asserted that the National Forest Management Act provides the basis for resolution of the crisis. Still needed, according to Harvey, are improved economic analysis of investments in and return on timber management, and additional research on nutrient depletion and other long-term effects of timber harvesting, maintenance of diversity of plant and animal species, and logging techniques which protect soil and water quality. Additionally, said Harvey, "We need to find ways of getting more diversity of viewpoints into decision-making."

Shands, William E., and Healy, Robert G. _The Lands Nobody Wanted: Policy for National Forests in the Eastern United States_. Washington, D.C.: The Conservation Foundation, 1977. 282pp.

This report evaluates public policy and management on the eastern National Forests. It grew out of a belief, held by The Conservation Foundation and others, that the _eastern_ National Forests constitute a distinctive segment of U.S. National Forest land and should receive increased, specialized attention directed toward their unique characteristics. Aimed at policymakers, legislators, forest managers, local officials, and the general public, the study incorporates a wide range of viewpoints obtained at four regional workshops sponsored by The Conservation Foundation.

The 49 eastern National Forests, comprising almost 24,000,000 acres, make up only 6.1% of all forested land in the East. Noting that 174 million people live within a day's drive of an eastern National Forest, the Foundation asserts, "these forests offer significant potential for satisfying local and regional environmental, economic and recreational needs." The report recommends that management be guided by two basic principles: (1) the eastern National Forests should provide public benefits not available from private lands; and (2) uses should be in harmony with restoring the forests as natural environments, distinct from the man-made environments otherwise dominant in the East.

The report places special emphasis on delineating the roles best suited to public and private capabilities. Accordingly, the authors suggest that the National Forests be targeted to producing superior hardwood and softwood timber requiring long growing cycles, and to low-intensity recreational uses, including temporary wildernesses in which timber management is limited to a final cut of mature timber. The authors also call for increased appropriations for forest acquisition.

Krutilla, John V., and Haigh, John A. _An Integrated Approach to National Forest Management_. Washington, D.C.: Resources For the Future, 1978. 41pp. (Reprinted from _Environmental Law_, Vol. 8, No. 2, 1978.)

This article is a thorough analysis of the Renewable Resources Planning Act as amended by the National Forest Management Act. The authors note what they term "internal inconsistencies" in the laws: (1) the culmination of mean annual increment as a harvest criterion can be inconsistent with efficient management; (2) limitations on timber removal could constrain efficient management; and (3) citizen participation can subvert the legislative intent by improper use of the process.

Four conclusions are drawn: (1) the function of a public resource management agency is to compensate for private or unregulated market failure; (2) a coherent management philosophy consistent with a benefit-maximizing criterion is required; (3) efficient resource allocation criteria should underlie legislation; and (4) implementation of the efficiency criteria contained in this legislation involves writing appropriate regulations and land use planning.

U.S. General Accounting Office. <u>The National Forests-Better Planning Needed to Improve Resource Management</u>. Washington, D.C.: U.S. General Accounting Office, 1978. 35pp.

This General Accounting Office (GAO) report was intended as a guide for the Forest Service in implementing the comprehensive planning required by the Forest Service and Rangeland Renewable Resources Planning Act of 1974 and the National Forest Management Act of 1976. The GAO review upon which the report was based was designed to improve Forest Service planning. Forty-two specific recommendations resulted.

The Forest Service was advised to incorporate into its new planning process careful definitions of planning levels (national, regional, forest) and assure that plans would be nationally standardized and prepared in sequence from the highest level down. GAO said it was essential that the Forest Service institute training programs and career incentives for planners. GAO also recommended that the Forest Service:

- increase its efforts toward interagency coordination;

- improve the linkages between planning and the budgeting/programming processes;

- strive for broad public involvement in the planning process.

Shands, William E. <u>Federal Resource Lands and Their Neighbors</u>. Washington, D.C.: The Conservation Foundation, 1979. 98pp.

Conducted for a consortium of seven federal agencies, including the USDA Forest Service, this study examined the conflicts between federal resource lands and neighboring private lands and communities. The study involved Washington interviews with federal officials and interest group leaders; questionnaires sent to federal land managers, state resource agencies, and timber companies; and field visits to seven areas. First, the study examined impacts to the federal lands from the activities of their neighbors. It then looked at the neighbors' perceptions of the federal lands.

Of most frequent concern to federal land managers were water quality impacts from a variety of development and agricultural activities; air pollution from urban sources and nearby industry; aesthetic impacts from low-quality strip development and powerlines; and pressures for uses of the public lands which conflict with the purposes of those lands.

Adjacent communities and landowners have differing perceptions of impacts from the federal lands. The extent of the influence of a federal unit, or its impacts on individuals and communities, is often judged by its neighbors on the basis of their expectations of economic gain. These expectations affect whether a community is receptive to the establishment of a new federal unit or the acquisition of additional land for an existing unit. Local interests often welcome the establishment of a federal unit which they anticipate will generate economic activity, or which they believe will insure availability of raw materials, such as timber or forage, essential to the local economy. Local interests are much more wary if they perceive that the federal land might be used for the environmental enhancement of the region--at the peril of regional economic development--or might be converted later from a "full use" area to one where locally important activities are discouraged or prohibited.

Among the report's conclusions:

- federal acquisition and land exchange procedures should be streamlined;

- state and local governments should improve their planning processes so that they can more effectively articulate state and local objectives;

- the federal agencies' resource management plans should describe the interrelationships between federal lands management and neighboring communities and private landowners, and propose actions to resolve conflicts;

- federal managers should be provided with more specific direction and given training in methods of reconciling conflicts.

Shands, William E.; Hagenstein, Perry R.; and Roche, Marissa T. <u>National Forest Policy: From Conflict Toward Consensus.</u> Washington, D.C.: The Conservation Foundation, 1979. 37pp.

This report reviews the controversies surrounding management of the nation's forested lands since the late 1800's, and explores ways in which the National Forest Management Act of 1976, through the planning process it mandates, might help resolve conflicts.

The authors see continued controversy over National Forest management issues, especially as regulations are developed governing amounts of timber to be cut, methods of harvest, and amounts of lands to be set aside as wilderness. Legal redress and appeals to Congress may still be part of the future, they conclude, but consensus might be reached in such areas as:

- the need to sustain both forest productivity and environmental quality;

- greater reliance on private, non-industrial woodlands for timber production;

- the need for increased forestry research; and

- an emphasis on intensive timber management on a relatively few highly productive National Forests as the Forest Service's commitment to help meet demands for timber.

The authors conclude that success in achieving consensus in forest management will depend largely on how well the planning process is used to strike a balance between flexibility in management to meet resource needs and stringency in protecting the environment.

VII: Policy for Non-Industrial Private Forests

The 1975 RPA Recommended Renewable Resource Program declared that "the biggest opportunity to increase timber growth" is on what have been termed non-industrial private forests--land owned by farmers and other private citizens. These small landowners hold 58 percent of the nation's commercial forest land. "Much of their land," said the Assessment, "is held for recreation, speculation, or other non-timber objectives, and little timber management is practiced at this time." This section reviews the major studies of the past decade aimed at exploring ways of increasing the supply of forest goods and services from non-industrial private forests (NIPFs). One document is the report of a task force organized by the American Forestry Association and National Association of Conservation Districts. Two other papers came out of a Resources for the Future conference on NIPFs. Because so little is known about the motivation of these landowners, we have included a Ph.D. thesis which seeks to establish an economic basis for projecting timber production for NIPFs. Also, we include the timber industry's program for increasing timber production on small private woodlands.

Pomeroy, Kenneth B., and Muench, John. <u>The Challenge of Private Woodlands: The Report of the Trees for People Task Force</u>. Rev. ed. Edited by Scot Butler. Washington, D.C.: American Forestry Association, 1975. 40pp.

The Trees for People Task Force was created in 1969 by the American Forestry Association and National Association of Conservation Districts. Comprised of 45 representatives of conservation organizations, industry, professional associations, and government agencies, it was charged with exploring the problems of the non-industrial private forests (NIPFs) and making recommendations for their solution. Its objective was to increase the productivity of NIPFs for all resources in order to meet the nation's resource needs and maximize landowner benefits.

The report describes the perspectives of the various interests represented on the task force, then offers recommendations by each interest group. The recommendations deal with such areas as education, motivation, and technical assistance to NIPF owners; tax changes and financial assistance; and manpower and equipment needs. Among the specific recommendations of the task force:

- forestry programs should be coordinated under a single agency at the community level to minimize red tape;

- the federal government should share in the cost of capital investments made by NIPF owners for the public

good, and should provide tax incentives and long-term
and emergency loans to owners;

- educational programs, owner cooperatives, and multiple-
use management plans should be encouraged.

In general, the report concludes that "the outlook for the owner
of the private, nonindustrial forest land is brighter today than
ever before" and that the public will be the long-run beneficiary
of actions taken to assist the NIPF owners in managing their
land.

Sedjo, Roger A., and Ostermeier, David M. <u>Policy Alternatives
for Nonindustrial Private Forests</u>. Report of the Workshop on
Policy Alternatives for Nonindustrial Private Forests,
sponsored by the Society of American Foresters and Resources
for the Future, Airlie, Virginia, August 30-September 1,
1977. Washington, D.C.: Resources for the Future and Society
of American Foresters, 1978. 64pp.

Thirty participants, representing a spectrum of forestry
backgrounds and interests, were invited to attend this workshop
to "take a fresh, critical look at the problems of nonindustrial
private forests (NIPFs), to identify the nature of the difficulties, and to explore policy alternatives for addressing these
ills." Discussion questions focused on the role of public funds
to stimulate output, the effectiveness of current public programs, the role of the forest products industry in stimulating
output, the impediments of taxation and environmental constraints, and government regulation. Four background papers were
presented by Marion Clawson, William Sizemore, Robert Manthy, and
Philip Raup. The conference participants were encouraged to
approach the questions innovatively, with unorthodox perspectives, and to think beyond the traditional views.

The authors state that the report is not a mirror of the
workshop proceedings. Rather, it is an analysis of some common
perceptions of NIPF problems, designed to stimulate futher
discussion and to explore several possible avenues for future
policy direction.

Several conclusions contrary to the traditional outlook
for timber supplies and NIPFs were generally agreed upon by the
participants:

- a future national timber shortfall is unlikely if prices
are allowed to increase at about their historical rate;

- when adjusted for regional differences, the fiber
productivity of NIPFs compares favorably with that of
the industrial forests and is superior to that of
National Forests; and

- if the economic function of NIPFs is viewed broadly, the highest value use for many NIPF's might not be wood fiber but outputs other than fiber, such as landowner amenities.

Five policy options are identified in the report. They include benign neglect; the status quo; modification and improved implementation of existing programs; market improvement by providing landowners with better information; and increased government involvement in the form of subsidies to landowners and government directives and regulation of forest practices. A synthesis or combination of two or three more policy alternatives with different responses at different government levels might offer an optimal policy mix, the authors conclude.

Clawson, Marion. *The Economics of U.S. Nonindustrial Private Forests*. Research Paper R-14. Washington, D.C.: Resources for the Future, 1979. 128pp.

The purpose of this report is to present "as accurate and as informative a description and analysis of the nonindustrial private forests (NIPFs) of the United States, as they are now and as they have changed over the past 25 years, as it is possible to do with the data available." The report, prepared as a background paper for a Resources for the Future and Society of American Foresters Symposium (see following report), contains much statistical information on NIPFs as well as an analytical framework for targetting public and private programs for NIPFs. Clawson's presentation (which includes commentary and a 91-page appendix of tables) substantially refutes or corrects historic misconceptions. The report shows that the "myths" that NIPFs are poorly stocked with growing timber, are seriously unproductive, practice poor forestry and are inefficient, have potential for greater output, and need public financial assistance are either wrong or overstated. Times have changed and the old ideas are inaccurate or less than accurate, Clawson argues.

Clawson postulates a classification of the states by economic potential of NIPFs based on the factors of biological productivity, inventory of kinds of trees (hardwoods and softwoods which are apt to be more in demand), and market opportunities. This will be useful, he says, in providing the basis for directing federal assistance programs toward areas with the greatest likelihood of increased productivity. Clawson places all of the Pacific Coast states and most of the South in the two top classifications with above-average economic potential for NIPFs.

Clawson includes an analysis of marketing and processing of timber from NIPFs. His background data reveal that "markets are seriously lacking for the species and grades of timber which they [the NIPFs] have grown," although he points out that adequate data are not presently available for a full consideration of markets and prices.

Because there is no detailed price reporting on a national scale, refined to fit local conditions, Clawson also suspects NIPF owners may be paid less for their stumpage than if competition were keener.

Regarding the economic potential of NIPFs' wood and other outputs, Clawson draws several conclusions:

- in general, harvest is less than growth on NIPFs, with softwood harvest outstripping that of hardwood because of better market opportunities;

- NIPFs are likely to produce more wood in the future than they do now and growth will continue to exceed harvests;

- the stimulus of higher prices would increase output, but this increased output from NIPFS would not be large in relationship to output which could be obtained from the National Forests if National Forests were managed on refined economic principles;

- in economic terms, gains in investment value seem by far the highest non-wood output of NIPFs; owners pursuing this objective will tend not to have an interest in forest management.

Binkley, Clark Shepard. "Timber Supply from Private Non-Industrial Forests: An Economic Analysis of Landowner Behavior." Ph.D. dissertation, Yale University, 1979. 127pp.

Non-industrial private forests have contributed significantly to national timber supply in the past and their contribution is expected to increase in the future, says Binkley, yet data which can be used for projections of NIPF supply have been weak. Binkley says his objective is to "quantify how timber prices, landowner and ownership characteristics, and the trade-offs between timber and non-timber forest outputs influence timber supply [from NIPFs]."

Since data regarding ownership characteristics and objectives on a national level are weak or non-existent, Binkley concentrates on quantitative analysis of the relationship between the price of timber and the probability of harvest among certain types of private, non-industrial owners in the Northeast. Binkley uses data from a sample of responses to a U.S. Forest Service survey of private, non-industrial forest land owners in New Hampshire. He also includes a qualitative analysis of interviews with participants in the Pilot Woodland Management Program, conducted in New England in the 1950's and 1960's.

Treating timber harvest as a utility function constrained by the owner's income and size of holding, Binkley constructs a formal, microeconomic model through which the relationship between timber price and harvest probability can be quantified, allowing for both timber and non-timber objectives. He formulates a supply equation as a function of stumpage prices, size of the holding, income and other socio-economic charcteristics of the owner, and the tradeoffs between timber and non-timber outputs. Among the study's major conclusions are:

- price is an important determinant of timber harvest (Binkley's finding of a 2.0-3.9 elasticity of harvest with respect to price contrasts with the Forest Service's estimate of a 0.5 elasticity); and

- farmers, less affluent owners, and owners of larger parcels are most likely to harvest timber.

Binkley recommends that public policies designed to increase output on NIPFs take these factors into account. He also suggests that non-timber outputs be given more weight in public policy. Realizing that the present data base is inadequate, Binkley calls for further statistical research on ownership objectives and on the technical tradeoffs between timber and non-timber outputs.

National Forest Products Association, Private Woodlands Committee. <u>America Grows on Trees: The Promise of Private Nonindustrial Woodlands</u>. Washington, D.C.: National Forest Products Association, 1980. 63pp.

Following up on the findings and recommendations of the Forest Industries Council's Forest Productivity Report (page 23), the Private Woodlands Committee of the National Forest Products Association sought to "define the private woodlands issue and develop positive policies for its resolution."

The need to stimulate timber production from the non-industrial forest sector is emphasized by a Forest Service study's findings that, in the South, 700,000 acres of softwood timber types are lost annually because the lands are not adequately regenerated with softwood species. Nationally, only one out of nine harvested acres on non-industrial forest is purposely regenerated. Of the opportunities to increase timber production identified by the Forest Productivity Report, 57 percent involving 78.7 million acres were on small private woodlands.

According to the forest industry, "private non-industrial lands must increase their share of the nation's timber supply from 42.3 percent in 1980 to approximately 50 percent by 2020 ... supplies must increase from 4.4 billion cubic feet to 8.3 billion cubic feet."

Industry's view, according to the report, "is that a basically free market system can yield needed wood supplies more efficiently and effectively than an approach which includes greatly increased government involvement and regulation of private land."

The report lists actions in research, program evaluation, communications, and information which industry feels should be undertaken by the federal government and recommends that government examine the effects of environmental regulations and land use restrictions on the productive management of private non-industrial forests, specifically regulations relating to water and air quality.

The report then sets forth recommendations for action by industry and the various levels of governments in three broad categories:

1. Economic incentives - These include investment tax credits, equitable estate taxation; a federally operated pilot forestry law program; and publicly funded cost share programs, which the report says "can stimulate forest management but should not be relied on as the sole solution to inadequate timber supplies."

2. Adequate technical assistance and contracted services - Individual companies need to increase programs to provide individual landowners with technical assistance to protect and manage their lands, the report asserts.

3. Communications, education, and motivation - This includes programs to educate and motivate small landowners, the development of a public climate "that accepts commercial, profit-oriented forestry as a means of meeting wood demand," and more effective communications programs by timber companies, industry associations, educational institutions, and public agencies.

The forest industry has established a Private Woodland Implementation Group to coordinate the program, emphasizing state level action. The goal is to implement the program before the 1985 update of the Forest Service RPA Program. "By then, on the ground results should be visible."

National Association of State Foresters and U.S. Department of Agriculture, Forest Service. <u>Proceedings of the National Private Non-Industrial Forestry Conference.</u> Sponsored jointly by the National Association of State Foresters and the U.S. Department of Agriculture, Forest Service, November 26-27, 1981, Washington, D.C. General Technical Report Wo-22. Washington, D.C.: U.S. Government Printing Office, 1981. 143pp.

This national conference culminated a year-long project on Private Non-Industrial Forestry involving a series of regional workshops and forums. The project sought to get "grass-roots" information on some of the 4 million small private forest landowners' needs and opinions. Forest Service officials, consultants, industry foresters, extension agents, and others were involved.

The conference developed nine categories of recommendations. They included:

- tax relief and incentives for landowners;

- technical assistance (from the forest products industry in particular);

- product market information;

- financial assistance (insurance, loans, and new approaches to existing subsidies);

- improved protection of forests from insects, disease, and fire;

- improved resource inventories;

- protection of landowners from risk of liability from public use of the land;

- minimal regulation; and

- better economic analysis of costs and benefits of forestry activities.

VIII: Forestry Research

There has not been a great deal of attention paid to forestry research needs during the past decade. In 1977 and 1978, the USDA Forest Service convened a series of meetings around the country to consider future forestry research directions, particularly for research conducted by the Forest Service or by land grant colleges with Forest Service funding. The proceedings of these meetings and resulting recommendations were published in 1978 in the Program of Research for Forests and Related Rangeland. In 1977, Resources for the Future convened a symposium on Research in Forest Economics and Forest Policy aimed at helping that organization develop its expanded forest research program; that symposium looked broadly at forest research needs. Earlier examination of various aspects of resources research dealt only peripherally with forestry topics. An advisory committee in 1972 looked at all Department of Agriculture research, and its report included a number of findings on Forest Service research. Finally, in connection with its study of the potential for increased use of renewable resources for industrial materials, another National Academy of Sciences committee looked at research needed to increase the supply of wood.

National Academy of Sciences, National Research Council. Report of the Committee on Research Advisory to the U.S. Department of Agriculture. Washington, D.C.: National Academy of Sciences, 1972. 464pp.

Formed at the request of the Secretary of Agriculture, Clifford M. Hardin, this Committee of basic and agricultural scientists was charged with advising USDA and the land grant universities on "gaps in scientific agricultural research and new advances that should be developed." In its report the Committee considered a number of issues, including whether the best dollar value was being obtained from funds spent on agricultural research, whether research conducted under USDA auspices was integrated with wider research in basic sciences, and whether high-quality scientists were being attracted to the Department's research programs.

The Committee concluded that USDA often devoted more funds and manpower to administration and planning than to actual research. It recommended that control over research be given to active researchers close to the project.

The Committee's evaluation of forestry research was based on the number of "messages" to the public about the research. It concluded that USDA and Forest Service research programs, particularly those using McIntire-Stennis funds, were relatively expensive ways of obtaining information. The overall conclusion was that the Forest Service does a good job, but other institutional arrangements for conducting forestry research might be more cost-effective.

Called the "Pound Report" after the Committee's Chairman, the report was widely criticized by USDA and Forest Service officials, who questioned the validity of its methodology, particularly the use of cost-per-message as a measure of research efficiency. An April 1973 Science magazine article quoted a high-ranking Agricultural Research Service official as saying the committee's report was "self-serving" and the committee's prime motivation was to get more funds for university researchers.

National Academy of Sciences, National Research Council, Commission on Natural Resources, Board of Agriculture and Renewable Resources, Committee on Renewable Resources for Industrial Materials. Renewable Resources for Industrial Materials. Washington, D.C.: National Academy of Sciences, 1976. 266pp.

In the belief that there was significant potential for renewable resources to be substituted for non-renewable resources in U.S. industrial production, the Office of Science and Technology Policy (OSTP) directed the National Academy of Sciences to "reexamine the role of renewable resources...in helping better to meet the needs for materials in the future." The Committee on Renewable Resources for Industrial Materials was directed to "undertake an analysis of renewable resources in the United States, identify the optimum production and use of such resources, and look at the role of science and technology in increasing their production and use."

Since wood is the principal renewable industrial material, many of the committee's recommendations deal with timber supply and production, with an emphasis on research needs.

Concerning supply of renewable resources, the Committee generally concluded that "the biological productivity (net realizable growth) of the commercial forest lands of the U.S. could be doubled within a half-century by the immediate and widespread application of proven silvicultural practices, provided economic and social conditions permit." The Committee recommended that USDA initiate research to evaluate opportunities to increase materials supply through more intensive forest management. Among the specific actions recommended were:

- USDA should improve the Forest Service's forest survey both in terms of aggregating data on a total forest basis and using more up-to-date sampling methods;

- USDA should conduct research into ownership objectives on non-industrial private forests and other socioeconomic aspects of forestry;

- USDA should establish production-scale demonstration tree farms to test various aspects of intensive management;

- USDA should cooperate with the Energy Research and Development Administration in evaluating opportunities for timber production to decrease dependence on external energy supplies.

Concerning production and use, the Committee found a need for increased research to spur the development of new technologies through which renewable resources could be substituted for nonrenewable. Recommendations were made for a number of government agencies, as well as the forest industry:

- OSTP should establish a center for renewable resource research;

- USDA and the Forest Products Laboratory should carry out research on the industrial use of agriculture-based materials;

- the National Science Foundation should sponsor university centers of research on renewable materials;

- the U.S. Agency for International Development should work with developing countries to increase their capacity to produce renewable materials;

- the Department of Commerce should develop a data bank to facilitate use of a "systems framework" in looking at materials;

- the major forestry corporations with research capability should "participate, as a matter of corporate policy, in research designed to produce published results."

On the basis of a projected increase in demand for new and reconstituted wood products, the Committee recommended research into the feasibility of:

- using forest residue to manufacture structural materials and to fuel mills;

- developing a non-petroleum based adhesive from lignin;

- developing new designs to lessen the weight of wood structure components.

Clawson, Marion, ed. <u>Research in Forest Economics and Forest Policy</u>. Research Paper R-3. Washington, D.C.: Resources for the Future, 1977. 555pp.

Presented at the symposium "Research in Forest Economics and Forest Policy" held in Washington, D.C. January 13-14, 1977, this collection of twelve papers was commissioned by Resources for the Future to assist in defining its research program.

The papers explore research needs and opportunities, describe the state-of-the-art in various research areas, and suggest directions for future research. A policy-oriented, interdisciplinary approach to research is empahasized throughout this volume.

General topics covered include:

- forestry in the setting of national economic policies;
- balancing resource supply and product demand;
- timber pricing;
- non-timber aspects of forestry;
- public/private interface;
- land use and multiple outputs;
- social issues;
- information resources;
- international economics;
- forest management; and
- policy issues.

The volume does not include a summary, but an overview prepared by Emery Castle attempts to identify gaps and priorities. Castle defines three basic criteria by which a research project should be selected: relevance, probability of success, and impact. He highlights several areas on which future research should be focused. These include:

- impacts of new forest technologies;
- factors influencing the economic instability of the forest industry;
- planning for multiple outputs; and

- factors influencing the flow of capital and labor into forestry.

Reinforcing the recommendation of contributor John Zivnuska, Castle suggests that rather than define international issues as separate research areas, researchers include an international component in all research questions. Recommendations of other authors regarding future research policies range from broad topics (balancing supply and demand, timber prices, taxation systems) to the very specific (effect of the Jones Act upon wood prices, evaluation of the efficiency of instituting a new Civilian Conservation Corps).

Lindmark, Ronald D., and Miller, Mason E., eds. National Program of Research for Forests and Associated Rangeland. Proceedings of a National Working Conference, January 17-19, 1978, Washington, D.C. Agricultural Reviews and Manual Series, ARM-H-1. Washington,, D.C.: U.S. Department of Agriculture, Science and Education Administration, August 1978. Paged variously.

This report combines seven separate publications, which document the findings of a two-year review of the content and conduct of forest and associated rangeland research conducted or sponsored by the Forest Service. The review formed part of a major regional/national planning effort called for by the USDA Agricultural Research Policy Advisory Committee.

Specifically, the publication includes the proceedings of the National Working Conference on forest and range research; the findings of the Research Policy Symposium, a meeting of 19 scientists and administrators convened by the Renewable Resources Foundation; the National Program of Research for Forests and Associated Rangelands prepared by a joint task force of the Department of Agriculture and National Association of State Universities and Land Grant Colleges; and four regional programs originating from the regional meetings.

The national program suggests a number of policy changes:

- place more emphasis on technology transfer;

- improve research planning and coordination, particularly by including other federal agencies and state and private organizations in the Current Research Information System (CRIS);

- achieve a better balance in research programs, both between research dealing with commodity and non-commodity resources and between basic and applied research.

The national conference and the regional conferences identified a number of research areas most likely to yield the greatest resource benefits:

- conversion of wood waste to sources of energy;
- pest and wildlife management;
- high-yield wood production from plantations;
- natural resource data improvement;
- soil/plant/water/nutrient relationships;
- improved management on non-industrial private forests;
- recycling waste materials on forest lands; and
- reclamation of surface-mined lands.

IX: International Forestry

Most of the reports surveyed for this section deal with forestry in developing or "Third World" nations, highlighting the intensive pressures on the forests to provide fuelwood and for conversion to cropland and resulting social, economic, and environmental problems. The first selection, however, deals with forest management in Canada, from which the United States gets a significant quantity of timber. Following selections address improved utilization of tropical forests; forestry in Third World countries; and the development of a United States policy for forest resources in tropical countries. The final report reviewed is the Global 2000 Report to the President prepared by the Council on Environmental Quality and the Department of State.

Reed, F.L.C., and Associates. Forest Management in Canada. Two vols. Information Report FMR-X-102 and FMR-X-103. Prepared for the Ottawa Forest Management Institute. Ottawa: Canadian Forestry Service, Environment Canada, 1978. Paged variously.

This report, prepared for the Canadian government's Forest Management Institute, examines the state of Canada's timber resource; potential supply and demand; and the current status--province by province--of forest management.

The report points out that timber comprises almost 20 percent of the nation's exports, much of which is sent to the United States. Canadian forestry programs are compared--unfavorably--with intensive management in the southern United States and Scandinavia. The study concludes: "At best, management is minimal and large areas receive little or no management because of a lack of commitment to forest management as a requirement for staying in business and a lack of funds for the necessary programs." The report contains a series of recommendations, including increased inventory data and research, more money for forestry, changes in the tax structure, and changes in the government institutions responsible for forestry. The report finds that "unless decisive action is taken immediately to advance intensive forest management, there will not be enough wood, the demands of the Canadian forest industry will not be satisfied and its competitive position in world markets will be weakened."

This report has caused timber companies and policymakers in the United States to question whether Canada will be able to maintain its level of exports to the U.S.

U.S. Department of Agriculture, Forest Service, Forest Products Laboratory. <u>Papers for Conference on Improved Utilization of Tropical Forests</u>. Sponsored by the U.S. Department of Agriculture, Forest Service Products Laboratory, and the U.S. Department of State, Agency for International Development, May 21-26, 1978, Madison, Wisconsin. Washington, D.C.: U.S. Government Printing Office, 1978. 442pp.

In order to disseminate information on the latest advances in the state of the art of tropical forest utilization, the U.S. Agency for International Development and the USDA Forest Service commissioned a series of papers for a 1978 conference on improved utilization of tropical forests. The papers covered the tropical forest resource; environment and silviculture; harvesting; transport and storage; wood fiber and reconstituted products research; industrial plans and practice; and investment considerations. Reflecting a broad spectrum of issues, individual papers treat subjects ranging from tropical forest biology to small forest industries in particular countries. Presentations focus on the results of silviculture experiments by governments, industry experiences with tropical woods, and the latest advances in wood fiber research as applied to the tropics.

The authors point out that removal of wood from tropical forests for commercial and industrial purposes (which represents a very small portion of the total wood removed) is characterized by removal of the best trees and species; vast quantities of underutilized secondary species which could represent significant potential for industrial development are left in the woods. Pilot studies indicate that the use of some tropical species for pulp and paper products is both technologically and economically feasible. Implementation of this research on a large scale could lead to improved forest management and the ability to produce more on less land.

Eckholm, Erik. <u>Planting for the Future: Forestry for Human Needs</u>. World Watch Paper 26. Washington, D.C.: World Watch Institute, 1979. 64pp.

This report is concerned with forest policies in response to societal needs for food, firewood, and timber in Third World countries. Unless these competing needs are balanced, deforestation, soil erosion, and desertification will increase, says Eckholm. He estimates that between 10 and 20 million hectares of forest land is lost each year in the less developed countries. But Eckholm believes that sound forestry measures could slow the pace of forest loss. Eckholm believes that decisions need to be made on investment priorities, land tenure systems, and technologies to be used. Among his recommendations:

- community-based forestry strategies, as opposed to large scale corporate plantation development, should be emphasized;

- agro-forestry systems should be instituted;

- conservation of forest products should be encouraged and substitutes for firewood developed.

The report describes innovative social forestry programs in China, South Korea, and the Indian state of Gujarat, which is cited as most progressive. Eckholm points to innovations such as the use of roadsides, canal banks, and idle lands for tree planting, the development and dissemination of wood-conserving cooking stoves, and small-scale cooperative tree farms as beneficial to less developed countries. He points out, however, that in social forestry "the problem is not so much what to do as how to do it."

U.S. Interagency Task Force on Tropical Forests. The World's Tropical Forests: A Policy, Strategy, and Program for the United States. Report to the President. Department of State Publication 9117. Washington, D.C.: U.S. Government Printing Office, 1980. 53pp.

An outgrowth of the United States Strategy Conference on Tropical Deforestation held in Washington, D.C. in June 1978, this report was presented to President Carter in response to his call for a U.S. strategy on tropical forests. The report attempts to place the issues of tropical forestry in their econmic and cultural context, balancing long-term goals against short-term subsistence needs of rural populations.

The United Nations Food and Agriculture Organization estimates tropical forest loss at approximately 12 million hectares per year. According to the report, drastic losses occur each year in tropical forests as a result of conversion to agriculture, fuelwood gathering (80 percent of wood removed from tropical forests is used for home cooking), and poor logging practices.

The report says that while the U.S. has less than one percent of the world's tropical forests, this nation has substantial political, economic, humanitarian, and other interests in preserving tropical forests.

The report lays out a national and international strategy for tropical forests:

- an international commitment to land management and cooperation;

- increased international research on tropical forests;

- renewed investment in reforestation and afforestation programs, including increased financial assistance from the U.S. for forestry programs in tropical countries;

- implementation of alternative technologies and programs designed to alleviate economic pressures which cause a drain on tropical forest resources;

- support of educational efforts aimed at increasing the capacity of local governments and institutions to protect their own resources;

- involvement of the private sector in all efforts.

Zerbe, John I; Whitmore, Jacob L.; Wahlgren, Harold E.; Laundrie, James F.; and Christophersen, Kjell A. <u>Forest Activities and Deforestation Problems in Developing Countries</u>. Report to the U.S. Department of State, Agency for International Development, Development Support Bureau, Office of Science and Technology. Prepared by the PASA Study Team for the U.S. Department of Agriculture, Forest Service, Forest Products Laboratory. Washington, D.C.: U.S. Government Printing Office, 1980. 194pp.

This report was commissioned by the U.S. Agency for International Development in cooperation with the Forest Service's Forest Products Laboratory. A five-person team was charged with assessing forestry activities in developing countries and making recommendations for combatting deforestation and improving forestry programs. The team's report, based on site visits to 17 developing countries, interviews with officials of U.S. and international aid agencies, and a review of relevant literature, describes current and proposed forestry projects in a number of developing countries.

While there is a great deal of industrial development using forest products, reforestation efforts are having a small impact relative to the severity of deforestation in developing countries. The authors find little emphasis on conservation and forestry education. Other problems which impede tropical forestry programs include expansion of shifting agriculture, high dependency on charcoal, insecure land tenure, and lack of forestry expertise.

The study concludes that despite some successes, the overall outlook for forestry in developing countries is grim. The authors make several recommendations for more successful forestry projects. Among them are:

- governments in developing countries and international agencies should increase their total commitment to forestry;

- communications among international agencies should be improved to better coordinate their activities;

- local participation should be built into all projects;

- increased support should be provided forestry education programs.

The study team also recommended that countries place greater emphasis on land use planning and agro-forestry, and implement programs to combat fuelwood shortages.

Barney, Gerald O. <u>The Global 2000 Report to the President: Entering the Twenty-First Century</u>. Three Vols. Volume I: The Summary Report; Volume II: The Technical Report; Volume III: The Government's Global Model. Prepared by the Council on Environmental Quality and the U.S. Department of State. Washington, D.C.: U.S. Government Printing Office, 1980. Paged variously.

In his environmental message to Congress in 1977, President Carter requested a study "of the probable changes in the world's population, natural resources, and environment through the end of the century." In response to this request, the Council on Environmental Quality and the State Department, with the cooperation of twelve federal agencies, carried out a three-year study to provide the foundation for the government's long-term environmental planning.

The Global 2000 study's principal findings generally are consistent, in spite of different assumptions, with five other global studies (the Latin American World Model, the World 2 and World 3 models used by the Club of Rome, the World Integrated Model, and the United Nations World Model). The report projects trends for global population, income, food, cropland, energy, forests, genetic resources, water resources, and air quality.

Forestry trends indicate that by the year 2000 forest cover and growing stocks of commercial-size wood will decline by 40 percent in less developed regions. The industrialized region's forests will decline by only 0.5 percent and growing stock by 5 percent. Deforestation is expected to continue until about 2020, when the world forest area will stabilize at about 1.8 billion hectares. At this time, all of the readily accessible forest in less developed countries is expected to have been cut. The real prices of wood products are expected to rise. In the less developed countries, where 90 percent of wood consumed is used for cooking and heating, this price rise could be catastrophic.

Environmental impacts also will be significant. Deforestation will result in soil erosion and desertification. Disturbance of forested watersheds affects water supply and contributes to the decline in renewable resource productivity. According to the report, the decline of the earth's carrying capacity could be widespread by the year 2000.

The report warns that "unless nations collectively and individually take bold and imaginative steps toward improved social and economic conditions, reduced human fertility, better management of resources, and protection of the environment, the world must expect a troubled entry into the twenty-first century."

RAYMOND H. FOGLER LIBRARY
DATE DUE
SUBJECT TO